"Frugality is an income."

Old English Proverb

WASHINGTON
Frugal Mania

A Money Saving Guide to the National Capital Area

WASHINGTON
Frugal Mania

A Money Saving Guide to the National Capital Area

Sarah Crim and Gwen Moulton

Capital Frugalist Press

Copyright © 1997 Capital Frugalist Press

All rights reserved; no part of this publication may be reproduced, stored in a retrieval system, or transmitted in any form by any means, electronic, mechanical, photocopying, recording, or otherwise, without the prior written permission of Capital Frugalist Press.

Manufactured in the United States of America
Second revised edition.
Library of Congress Catalog Card Number 96-85487
ISBN: 0-9653092-0-7
Cover design: Fahey & Associates
Index: David Noss

Library of Congress Cataloguing-in-Publication Data

Crim, Sarah
　　Washington frugal mania : a money saving guide to the national capital area / Sarah Crim and Gwen Moulton
　　Includes index.
　　ISBN 0-9653092-0-7
　　　　　　　　　　　　　　　96-85487

Capital Frugalist Press
16010 Pennsbury Drive
Bowie, Maryland, 20716
(301) 249-3755

To all who strive to be thrifty and thrive

Contents

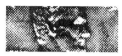

Preface	xi
Acknowledgments	xvii

Chapter 1
Food for Frugal Thought ... 1

Chapter 2
Frugal Fashions ... 21

Chapter 3
Home Frugal Home ... 47

Chapter 4
Just for Kids (of All Ages) ... 71

Chapter 5
Entertainment, Special Days ... 89

Chapter 6
Treasure Hunting ... 115

Chapter 7
Community Focuses ... 135

Appendix ... 165

Index ... 167

Frugal Maniac Attack

Preface

THIS BOOK IS A FRUGALITY GUIDE for Washington metropolitan-area residents as well as for visitors. It can save you large amounts of money. It is for those who want to be able to weather with aplomb budgetary storms such as the furloughs and downsizings of 1995, or other economic hazards we now know can occur here, in the formerly recession-proof national capital area. This book also can be used as a guide for those who want to lower their short-term costs while visiting, or temporarily living, in one of the highest cost-of-living areas in the country.

In other words, this volume is for anyone who wants to incorporate the principles of frugality into their lives to cut spending in some areas so that their paychecks are channeled into other areas that are personally important to them. Newcomers to the metro area as well as long-time residents will find helpful information, as will college students, newlyweds, retirees, singles, and families.

In our years of teaching classes on how to live frugally in the D.C. area, and in the pages of our newsletter, *The Capital Frugalist,* we showed our students and readers that there are great (not just good) bargains to be found in the metro area on food, clothing, furniture, entertainment and a variety of other necessities and luxuries. Washington is an especially good place to live well while being frugal, and in the pages of this book, we show you how to take advantage of the options available to save potentially thousands of dollars per year without feeling deprived.

We are two professional journalists—and native Washingtonians—with more than 25 years of wide-ranging reporting experience between us. We believe, in fact, that it is often fun to be frugal— the thrill of the chase for bargains, the joy of victory in saving money and then using it for the things you truly want, and yes, the agony of defeat when you recall the good deals that got away.

Frugal mania has hit Washington like never before. Here, you can find scores of yard sales every weekend between April and November in D.C., Maryland, and Virginia; there are more resale consignment stores in business than ever before, specializing in everything from clothing and furniture to sporting equipment and books; flea markets around the region are common; and government surplus sales and other offshoots of this town's number one employer are abundant.

Washingtonians are ready to be frugal. In the mid-1990s, the federal government weathered downsizings, closings, and finally in late 1995 and early 1996, back-to-back furloughs of several hundred thousand employees that left these workers without paychecks right around the holidays. Federal employees, federal contractors, and a myriad of other local businesses felt powerful economic shockwaves akin to those that other parts of the country have experienced for many years. The ripple effects on the entire local economy were considerable. Area residents found that while some creditors were sympathetic, some were not. However, workers who had a cushion of emergency savings and little or no debt definitely fared better in the shutdown than did overextended, paycheck-to-paycheck households.

Students in our classes have told us about many obstacles they have encountered in trying to be more frugal. Among these are: time, self-discipline, family resistance, location, fear of what other people will think, addictive patterns, and lack of information. This book primarily seeks to address the last obstacle by arming readers with the type of sources and useful techniques they can apply to reach their goals. In so doing, we have saved readers innumerable hours of research time.

Sure, frugal living takes some time, but so does everything else in life. And once a person starts down the frugal path, he or she tends to become ever more creative in generating new ways to save. Time management experts tell us that as few as 10 minutes per day of planning can lead to much greater efficiencies in the use of our precious time and energy.

Frugal living involves planning, patience, and

a willingness to be driven by one's goals and not one's ego, to ensure that hard-earned dollars go where they can do you the most good and make you happier. There can be both long-term and short-term value in frugality, from enabling people to handle current significant financial outlays such as vacations, to managing future plans such as saving for college or retirement. We see this "frugal mania," therefore, as empowerment, not deprivation.

A recent study showed that Washingtonians work some of the longest hours of any U.S. metropolitan area's residents. Harvard economist Dr. Juliet Schor in her acclaimed 1991 book, *The Overworked American*, found that many Americans are working longer hours or extra jobs to acquire consumer goods that they may not want or need. She also observed that one's life is made up of the hours that are in it, not the things that are in it. When we spend less money on the things in our lives, we may be able to work fewer hours, and thus give ourselves more time to use those hours in ways that give our lives personal meaning and satisfaction, according to Schor.

Personal satisfaction and choices are what this book is all about. The authors are not financial experts, but have gained their knowledge through experience, study, and hands-on shopping. We have strived to include a wide range of shops, events, activities, and facilities for the frugal-minded. We do not claim, however, to have covered every frugal destination in the Washington area.

The principles of frugality are an excellent tool for crafting your life the way you want it to be, and we have covered a large segment of topics in this book so that you can pick and choose to incorporate these principles to fit your lifestyle. We hope the result will be fewer debts, less stress, more time for yourself, and a shield when economic times get rough.

Go ahead, enjoy a frugal maniac attack.

Sarah Crim and Gwen Moulton
October 1996

Acknowledgments

WE APPRECIATE THE HELP OF MANY PEOPLE who helped make this book possible through their moral support; their time; and their hard work:

Tim Fahey of Fahey & Associates, Washington, D.C., a marketing, communications, and graphics design company, for his cutting-edge and creative design work on the cover, his suggestions for design elements throughout the book, and his invaluable penny;

Playwright Eliot Byerrum for insightful comments and advice on the manuscript;

Deb Leopold, president of First Class Inc., the Washington continuing education center where we first launched, and then over the years refined, our knowledge about and our interactions with the frugal set;

Jennifer Kinsey for imparting knowledge about designing corporate workshops and other important areas;

The people who allowed us to interview them and provided a plethora of information;

Numerous people we met along the way who told us to go for it;

And of course, our husbands, children, parents, and extended families, who let us take the precious hours necessary to pull this book together when we and they sometimes would have preferred to be out playing.

Food for Frugal Thought

Chapter 1

FOOD IS ONE OF THE BIGGEST PORTIONS of the average household budget. It's truly one of those things that you cannot live without. In the Washington metro area it seems that time costs money, at least when it comes to eating. Busy Washingtonians grab a quick donut or bagel for breakfast in the company cafeteria, get lunch at a carryout, and often order in for dinner because there's no one sufficiently un-tired at the end of the day to cook.

The only family anyone sees sitting down to a home-cooked meal every night seems to be the 1950s sitcom family the Cleavers on cable TV, viewed over a plate of Chinese takeout or a pizza by the harried 1990s family.

A front-page story in the March 15, 1995 *USA Today* noted a food industry survey that found 47 percent of people say they eat out because they "haven't time to prepare food at home." This was the reason most frequently given; it was followed by the 18 percent who said they "don't want to cook." A mere 5 percent of survey respondents said they eat out to celebrate an occasion (remember when the latter was the main reason to go out to eat?)

It does not have to be thus. Frugalists who have mastered the basic principles of buying groceries inexpensively as put forth in this chapter are just as susceptible as anyone else to buckle in to fatigue or the lateness of the hour and go out, or order in for dinner, thus negating the value of those low-cost groceries.

Besides the savings in time, there are considerable savings in money when one eats at home, especially compared to restaurant and carryout prices. For instance: takeout Chinese food for a family of four will cost about $20. Chicken sliced from a Sunday roaster and stir-fried with frozen vegetables and rice at home will cost less than $5, maybe only $3 to $4 if the chicken and vegetables were purchased on sale. Moneywise, there's no comparison (there's also no MSG).

Key principles, local deals

This chapter offers a simple strategy for cutting food costs by focusing on homemade meals and offering tips on local stores' deals. We call it "The Frazzled Frugalist's Strategy for Placing Home-Cooked Food on the Table." This strategy requires a little advance planning, but it saves time, money, and nerves (it is both kitchen- and nerve-tested).

This plan is simple and effective. It saves time and money, plus it allows you to control the quality of your meals, as well as food health factors such as fat and salt content. Here are the basics: 1) Prepare to shop 2) Prepare to cook 3) Shop using frugal tactics 4) Cook using frugal methods.

We all know that grocery shopping, like death and taxes, is inevitable and everpresent. But grocery shopping in the Washington, D.C. area does not have to take a huge bite out of your income.

There are some excellent ways to cut the costs of food shopping, and various supermarkets in the metro area have different methods of pricing and marketing of which consumers can take advantage.

Plan your trip first by using some general principles that will result in significant savings on food at the grocery store, even if you go to the most expensive place in the neighborhood. Here they are:

Prepare to shop

Carefully check the food section of the newspaper(s), as well as supermarket circulars that come to you in the mail, to see what is on sale that week.

When you go shopping, make a list and stick to it as much as possible. Impulse purchases can wreck your grocery bill—and yes, it's true, do not go shopping on an empty stomach and avoid bringing your children when possible.

Inventory what you already have and then stock up—to the degree your household space comfortably allows—on those sale items that are staples in your household. Since sales seem to run in cycles of about four to six weeks in the grocery stores, you can arrange things so that by the time you're running low on an item, it's on sale again. Multiply this principle as much as possible throughout your grocery shopping, and it really adds up over a year's time.

Clip coupons on items you would use anyway (Sunday papers, magazines, mailers). Combining coupons with sales is an especially good way to save. Giant, Safeway, Weis, Magruder's, as well as other markets, often have weekly half-price and third-off specials, and offer double the face value of coupons as well.

For example: Using the stock-up principle, during the first week of October 1994, if you saved the $1 coupon for Kellogg's Corn Flakes that was in the newspaper a few weeks earlier, you could combine it with Magruder's half-price special of an 18-ounce box of the product for $1.29, to obtain that box for 29 cents. Those are 1940s prices! It's not 25 cents a bowl, like in the Kellogg's commercial, it's about 3 cents a bowl! (okay, 7 cents, with the milk.)

Shop using frugal tactics

Consider buying the lowest-cost version of an item. For example, if you love premium orange juice and buy a $3.00 half-gallon container of it every week, you might consider buying a 12-ounce frozen can of that premium juice for $1.49 (this makes 48 ounces)—or stocking up on it when Giant or Magruder's or another store puts it on sale, usually for $1.19.

Or you could buy a house brand of frozen orange juice for 99 cents—or stock up on the house brand on sale (we've seen this last version for as low as 59 cents). On just this one item, over a year's time, the highest price version described here will cost slightly under 5 cents per ounce and the lowest cost version is a little over 1 cent per ounce. For those families where a great deal of juice is consumed, the savings can amount to hundreds of dollars per year.

Buy fewer processed foods. Get 10 pounds of potatoes for $1.59 and cut them up and fry them yourself, rather than buying one pound of frozen french fries for $1.00. Ten pounds of the frozen product is $10, and one pound of the bag potatoes is less than 16 cents! It doesn't take that much more (if any) time to fry or bake (8 minutes in the microwave) your own. This example shows a savings of 84 percent between frozen and bagged. The less processed, the less packaged, the less advertised a product is, the less it costs. So fresh vegetables and fruits, in season, on sale, save very large amounts of money. Buy enough to meet your needs; freeze leftovers to avoid waste.

Use unit pricing. Warehouse stores have those huge sizes of everything, for example, but your calculator may show you that the best buy is a smaller size. The per-ounce, per-pound, per-whatever cost, is very telling, so bring your calculator whenever you go grocery shopping, or check the unit prices that stores usually post with the item price on the shelving.

Eat less meat and when you do, buy cheaper cuts of meat. Meat can be a major food expense. Stock up on sale meat and freeze it, buy meat from the "just about to expire bin" and freeze it or cook immediately to ensure it doesn't spoil.

Combine sale/coupon/less processed foods to make much less expensive meals. After you've begun to stock up on things, you can put together your sale purchases to make much cheaper meals.

You can make a quick stir fry with sale-purchased meat and vegetables (frozen vegetables if you're time-pressed and don't want to chop them up); 33-cents-a-bag pasta with a jar of spaghetti sauce you got on sale with a coupon, maybe some sale ground beef browned and thrown into the sauce. These are quick meals and there is no need to send out for expensive carryout (waiting for carryout takes time, too).

Avoid the impulse-buying trap. Supermarkets are set up to get you to buy their most high-profit merchandise. That merchandise is always highly visible, at eye level, or in a place you have to pass through as you wend your way toward that gallon of milk that brought you into the store in the first place.

Supermarkets, co-ops, specialty groceries

Don't hesitate to let food chains' corporate headquarters or your local grocer know how you feel about their policies, good or bad. It is through feedback from the public that policies are changed. The list below

---

More signs of the frugal times . . .

"Consumers saved $2.1 billion by using manufacturer's coupons in the first half of 1995."
(Hey, that's more than a few bucks. The average face value of the coupons was 67 cents. But the number of people redeeming coupons was 5 percent lower than the previous year. Factoids courtesy of *Editor & Publisher* magazine, Aug. 5, 1995.)

"The U.S. grocery industry brings in revenue of $400 billion, two-thirds of which comes from impulse buys."
(From an article in the *Washington Post*, Aug. 21, 1995, on the concept of grocery shopping from home. The costs range from $7 to $15, but consumers are reported to be still willing to drive to save the delivery service fees.)

is not all-inclusive, but enumerates the major grocery store chains in our area, selected cooperatives and specialty markets.

- Shoppers Food Warehouse, Corporate headquarters 4600 Forbes Blvd., Lanham, Md. 20706; (301) 306-8600.
- Bethesda Co-op, 6500 Seven Locks Rd., Cabin John, Md. 20817; (301) 320-2530. 5,000-square foot store catering to vegetarians. No meats; stocks organic and non-organic produce; 150 bulk items. For $30 per year membership fee, one receives a 5 percent discount on food. "Working members" who donate three hours per week (stocking shelves, parceling food, etc.) get a 15 percent discount. Coupons accepted, but no doubling.
- Caribbean Market II, 7505 New Hampshire Ave., Langley Park, Md. 20783; (301) 439-5288. Good inexpensive source of spices (many sold in large bags).
- Co-op Supermarket, 121 Centerway, Greenbelt, MD 20770; (301) 474-0522. 11,000-square feet. Set up like traditional grocery store. One-time membership fee of $10 entitles one to annual rebate check based on percentage of profits. Double coupons.
- Whole Foods Stores (formerly) Fresh Fields Markets, Corporate headquarters 4948 Boiling Brook Parkway, Rockville, Md. 20852; (301) 984-3737.
- Giant Food, Inc. 6300 Sheriff Rd., Landover, Md. 20785; (301) 341-4100.

- Glut Food Co-op, 4005 34th St., Mt. Rainier, Md. 20712. Small natural food store; vegetarian; low prices (301) 779-1978. Special program: Every Sunday morning one can sign up to work a shift during the coming week as a volunteer (shifts are 8 a.m. to 1 p.m., 1 p.m. to 5 p.m., and 5 p.m. to 8 p.m.). In return one gets $4.25 per hour in "food scrip" that can be used to buy groceries in the store, up to a maximum of $600 per year.
- Magruder's Grocery, Corporate Offices 981 Rollins Ave., Rockville, Md. 20852; (301) 230-3000.
- Bethesda Farm Women's Cooperative Market, 7155 Wisconsin Ave., Bethesda, Md. 20814; (301) 652-2291.
- Safeway Stores Inc. Division offices for Washington, D.C. area. 4551 Forbes Blvd. Lanham, Md 20706; (301) 918-6500.
- Katz Kosher Super Market, 4860 Boiling Brook Parkway, Rockville, Md. 20852; (301) 468-0400.
- Weis Markets, Corporate headquarters, 1000 South Second St., Sunbury, Pa. 17801; (717) 286-4571.

Different local deals

Warehouse stores such as Price Club and Sam's Club can offer great deals on large-size versions of items, but make sure you really want that 12-pound jar of dill pickles—if it goes to waste, it's not a bargain. And always check the unit pricing at these stores—sometimes the largest-size item is *not* the

> ### Food storage and handling
>
> Invaluable and free sources of information to protect your food investment, once you get it home, include:
>
> **U.S. Department of Agriculture, Food Safety and Inspection Service, pamphlet** on proper freezing techniques and length of time foods can remain frozen, contact: Consumer Information Catalog Pueblo, Colo. 81009
>
> **USDA's Meat and Poultry Hotline (800) 535-4555,** Mon.-Fri.,10-4 p.m. for personal advice, or 24-hour recorded food safety messages on current topics, seasonal information, advice handling food related to a power failure, product recalls, nutrition, and cooking equipment.
>
> **Giant Food Inc. pamphlets** on safe food handling, available at all store locations.

best buy.

In general, Giant and Safeway tend to be more expensive overall than the smaller chains nipping at their heels, such as Magruder's and Shopper's Food Warehouse. But every store has its own strengths.

Giant's bulk foods bins are good for frugalists, because many of the items are cheaper (to varying degrees) than their boxed counterparts elsewhere in the store. Also, there is less waste, because you can buy only as much as you need. Every week Giant puts some of its bulk foods on sale (either 1/3 or 1/2 off). Particularly during the holiday season, a large number of baking goods such as nuts, raisins, and candies are obtainable at very good prices this way. The bins are definitely worth checking out for a wide range of items. This is especially true for staples such as rice and cereal if you have a large family. (There are even helpful tear-off cooking instructions located near the bins.) Remember to slap the bin sticker code on your bag, so it can go through the scanner.

Giant offers double coupons up to 50 cents value, and has half-price, third-off, and 15 percent off specials each week. Coupon/sale/stock up combination strategies work well at Giant. In the past, sale item purchases usually were limited to six items, but the chain seems to have lifted this policy for now.

Some type of bread is usually put on half-price sale each week, and day-old baked goods are usually fairly plentiful and fresh. Their Superdeals, large-size containers, came into being to compete with the warehouse stores. Sometimes these are good buys, but they often are name-brand, highly advertised goods, so those advertising/packaging costs are still in there.

Safeway has its Savings Club (lower prices for members; no fee required) and does not put limits on the quantities of sale items you can purchase. The store also offers double coupons up to 50 cents face value. But remember to bring your membership card or you're stuck with the higher, non-member prices. Check the about-to-expire bins early in the morning at the meat department. A variety of meats are available if you hit it on the right day (each store varies, so check to see how the Safeway in your neighborhood does it).

Shoppers Food Warehouse and Magruder's usually have lower-cost produce than Safeway and Giant, and generally seem to be a few cents cheaper on just about everything else, which by some estimates can mean regular savings of 10 percent to 15 percent on the total food bill over the larger chain stores. Magruder's has one-day specials

($1.99 for milk on Tuesday, for example) in the Sunday paper for Sunday through Tuesday specials, and Wednesday paper for Wednesday through Saturday specials. Magruder's doubles coupons up to 50 cents face value, and single value after that. Shoppers takes coupons, but offers no doubling.

Another hint for savings: Ethnic markets and farmer's markets often sell exotic spices and certain staple foods such as rice much more cheaply than the small bottles and packages one finds in the chain supermarkets.

With the costs associated with year-end holidays always a large budget item, it is always a good time to keep one's eyes open for sales on nonperishable food items you can use during the holiday season to hold down the cost of holiday entertaining, such as coffee in cans; tea; and baking mixes.

Example: an oatmeal discovery

In an expedition to check out prices for that winter staple, quick-cooking oatmeal, we found in 1995 that the price for this product and indeed, many other products, can vary tremendously, even within the confines of one store. Here's the scoop:

a) Giant—Quaker Oats brand quick oats, **18 ounce box $1.99; $1.77 per pound.**

b) Giant—(store brand) Super G Quick Oats, **18 ounce box $1.39; $1.24 per lb.**

c) Giant—Super G Quick Oats, **42 ounce box $2.79; $1.06 per lb.**

d) Magruder's—Quaker Oats, **42 ounce box $2.98; $1.14 per lb.**

e) Magruder's—(store brand) Nature's Best quick oats, **42 ounce box $2.48; 94.5 cents per pound**

f) **BEST BUY**—Giant bulk foods bin, **59 cents per pound** (this is the regular price for this item).

Equivalent of an 18-ounce package of oatmeal would be 67 cents. A 42-ounce package would be $1.54, only 15 cents more than the Giant store brand 18-ounce box!

The oatmeal, according to the bin sign, was $1.20 per pound less than a comparably priced product (we guess they were comparing it to the most expensive version, the 18-ounce box of Quaker Oats). Co-op markets often have bulk foods bins as well (see listing later in this chapter).

We have found that use of the principles enumerated above can save a family $1,000-$1,500 per year over previous grocery costs. It takes about two hours per week to read the papers, clip coupons, inventory what you already have, and make the shopping list, but on an annual basis the savings are worth it. Who would turn down an annual raise of $1,500?

Prepare to cook and cook it up

√ Decide how much time you can realistically devote to cooking. As the examples below show, some people cook meals for nearly every day of the week. Others can only manage two or three. It is up to you, given your lifestyle, how much improvement you want to make over your current situation.

√ Cook way ahead of time. The *Bowie* (Md.) *Blade News* ran a story in 1995 about two neighbors who get together once a month, cook 70 meals in one day, divide the meals so each of their families gets half, and then freeze. Their plan is based on guidelines suggested in the book, *Once-a-Month Cooking*, by Mimi Wilson and Mary Beth Lagerborg, Focus on the Family Publishing, Copyright 1993, Word, Inc. (800) 933-9673. The neighbors say this method saves unbelievable amounts of time, although we noted that once exhumed from the freezer, some of the pre-cooked meals required 40 minutes to an hour in the oven before they were ready.

√ Or try to cook at least three or four days ahead at a time. If one does not want to or cannot cook a month ahead, we advise cooking several days ahead in order to avoid that recurring weekday thought, "Omigosh what'll we have for dinner? I'm too tired to cook." One can use the ingredients one has stockpiled—often on sale—in the cupboard or freezer to make dishes that can be quickly heated up as the week progresses, and as leftovers, make good lunches. Sunday evenings or late afternoons—after outings for the weekend are completed—are a good time to do this.

One can have two casseroles cooking in the oven and something on top of the stove at the same time, thus saving time and energy (both yours and the stove's). Note: Even more energy dollar savings are achieved by cooking on Sunday afternoon if you live in a jurisdiction where "time-of-day" electrical rates are reduced on weekends. For example, Baltimore Gas & Electric Co. "high savings" rates, in effect all weekend long, are about 65 percent less than peak rates. So the oven—a high energy user—is used minimally and at minimal cost, while the foods prepared in advance can be reheated quickly in the more energy-efficient microwave oven.

 These Sunday-concoction dishes then can be pulled out on Monday, Tuesday, and Wednesday nights; and any leftovers can become lunches. Old standbys—tuna, salmon, or chicken mixed with noodles or rice, sliced-potatoes in casseroles, pasta mixed with ground beef and spaghetti sauce, lasagne, stews, pot roast, a roasted chicken that can be cut up and stir-fried later in the week—all of these recipes work well this way. The cooking takes about two to three hours (during which time you can do other things besides watch the ingredients heat and blend), and then the dishes can cool, be covered, and go into the fridge or freezer until they are called to duty. When one comes home tired on a Tuesday, that "heat and eat" tuna casserole will look mighty good to everyone—and it will be ready to eat in about 10 minutes, leaving a much larger portion of the evening free for other things.

 √ Focus on one-dish meals when possible. One person we know buys canned mushroom soup whenever it's on sale because it makes a good "binder" sauce for casseroles (as do sour cream, cream sauces, and spaghetti sauce.) Fortunately for the frugalist mindset, not only do most casseroles taste as good or better the next (or next next) day, their ingredients are inexpensive to begin with and often on sale: for example, tuna, ground beef, pasta, pasta sauce. In making these types of meals regularly, it's a good idea to stock plenty of these ingredients to create your own "mix and match" casseroles.

√ Keep frozen vegetables on hand. These are nutritionally superior to the canned variety, and are near-equal nutritionally to fresh vegetables, dietitians say. Giant's Superdeals section often has four-pound bags of a broccoli/cauliflower/carrot blend (all three of these vegetables are rated by the Center for Science in the Public Interest as among the highest in nutritional value; they also have few calories) on sale for about $4. A saucepan full of these vegetables takes just a few minutes to steam and complements a casserole nicely. Safeway often puts its Bel-Air brand of frozen veggies on sale. There is no waste using these vegetables, because they don't spoil, and are quick to cook.

√ Remember the value of leftovers. (This is a true frugalist theme, as this book will show over and over again.) When you cook dinner, make extra and bring to work for lunch the next day. Those microwaveable lunches at the grocery store may look inexpensive at first glance, but at $3 a pop, they can't hold a candle savings-wise to your leftover dinner of comparable portion, which is probably at least 75 percent cheaper. The frozen, processed entrees, however, can be cheaper than many restaurant lunchtime meals, which often *start* at

$10 downtown. So, weigh your own situation accordingly. Put the leftovers in plastic containers that can be taken along for lunches the next day. Be sure to keep plenty of containers on hand (always snap-uppable at yardsales for 10 cents or 25 cents), since they have a tendency to disappear at the office, in the car, occasionally melt down in the microwave, or lose their tops.

√ Keep around food that's "good to grab" if you usually are rushed in the morning. Yogurt, fresh fruit such as oranges and bananas, granola bars, graham crackers, fruit/fig bars, and popcorn can be grabbed and stashed in a bag to take to work in a matter of seconds if you're in a rush to get a child to school on time or make a bus or train. If it's not enough food to get you through the day, you may have to supplement, but at least you won't have to buy all of breakfast and all of lunch. (It's best to pack lunches the night before, if you can.)

Discount bakeries listing

A number of bakeries that supply goodies to the local grocery stores have what they call thrift outlets. These are stores where slightly older (but still delicious and nutritious) or overstock items, such as bread, cakes, and pastries, are sold to the public at a discount.

• Entenmann's Bakery, 1327-A Rockville Pike, Rockville, Md. (301) 762-1215; hours Tues through Fri 9-6; Sat, Sun, Mon 9-5.

• Pepperidge Farm Thrift Store, 15513 New Hampshire Ave., Silver Spring, Md. (301) 384-

4420. Mon-Fri 9:30-6, Sat 9-5:30, Sun 11-4.

• Pepperidge Farm Thrift Store - 7309 MacArthur Blvd., Bethesda, Md. (301) 229-0953. Mon-Wed 9:30-6:30, Thurs and Fri 9:30 to 8; Sat 9:30-5:30, Sun 9:30-4.

• Wonder/Hostess Bakery Thrift Store, 11400 Baltimore Ave., Beltsville, Md. (301) 937-8080, Mon-Fri 9-7, Sat 9-5, Sun 10-4.

• Wonder Bread Thrift Store, 5820 Seminary Rd., Baileys Crossroads, Va. (703) 820-2746; Mon-Fri 9-7, Sat 8-6, Sun-10-4.

• Wonder Bread Thrift Store, 52nd Ave. & Addison Chapel Rd., Beaver Heights, Md. (301) 773-6565; Mon-Fri 9:30-5:30; 9:30-5 Sat, closed Sun.

• Wonder Bread Thrift Store, 1175 Taft, Rockville, Md. (301) 424-4901; Mon-Fri 9-6; Sat 8-5; closed Sun.

FTC warns about scanner pricing

Besides shopping carefully for the best prices, remember to make sure the prices get rung up that way at the register. A brochure issued by the Federal Trade Commission in mid-1995 tells consumers to watch out for electronic price scanners at the grocery store and other checkout counters because they often overcharge.

According to the brochure, *Attention All Shoppers: Make Sure the Scanned Price is Right*, consumers should: double-check prices at the checkout counter using the store's sale flyer; take note of special deals in the store; and complain to the manager if there seems to be a pattern of overcharging on items that are supposed to be on sale. (Note: some stores, such as Giant, have a policy of giving the customer one of the items for free, if the scanner overcharges and the customer calls it to the store's attention.)

Consumers should also report to the state attorney general, and/or the local or state consumer affairs office recurring problems at particular stores, the FTC advised. In many cases, scanners are used in place of price tags on individual products, so the consumer should be watching carefully at the check-out counter, the agency said. While retailers say the electronic scanners have improved customer service and result in fewer pricing errors than manual pricing, some consumer groups estimate that scanner errors can cost consumers millions of dollars annually.

A copy of the brochure and other consumer advisories can be obtained from FTC Public Reference Branch, Room 130, 6th and Pennsylvania Ave., N.W., Washington, D.C. 20580; (202) 326-2222.

Voice from past echoes in the present

In our journeys to thrift shops, we are always quick to pick up an old book for 25 cents or 50 cents that might offer some thrifty hints that are sometimes so old they are mostly now forgotten. While, for the price, even one or two hints from such a book would make it worth buying, we came upon a real gem — a cookbook written in 1937, during the heart of the Great Depression, called

The Most for Your Money Cookbook, by Cora, Rose and Bob Brown (Modern Age Books, New York).

The tone of the book is not unlike that set by President Franklin D. Roosevelt in his 1937 inaugural address: "We have always known that heedless self interest was bad morals; we know now that it is bad economics."

What made this book especially interesting was the fact that some of the problems the authors referred to concerning modern Americans' need to be thrifty—and of course the need was very great when they wrote this book—are *still* with us.

We'd like to share a few of the authors' salient points on personal economics, with references to the present, when appropriate. As the French say, "Plus ca change, plus c'est la meme chose"— the more things change, the more they remain the same. Some of the quotes that follow show that some things have indeed changed little.

Interesting cooking substitutions when ingredients are unavailable: "Few cooks know the advantage of snow as an ingredient, yet a cup of freshly fallen snow actually takes the place of two eggs in making a pudding light and toothsome...[with] a finer texture because of the chemicals released in melting—some say it's the ammonia. (Nowadays, better check your local air quality before using this free ingredient).

Throwing away food: "Thrifty Europeans, who, as a rule, live better than we do on less, claim that we throw away more than we eat, and that comes too close to the truth to be any comfort to our intelligence." They still say that about us.

Homemade soup: The authors offer this recipe for "Economy Soup" that sounds somewhat tasty. "Boil a minced onion in 1 1/2 quarts stock or water, with a cup of bread crumbs. Press all through a sieve. Bring to boiling point and season. Remove from fire and stir in 2 egg yolks beaten with a couple of tablespoons milk. Sprinkle grated cheese over each plate after serving."

Small amounts of product in big packages: A major network nightly news report recently noted the widespread phenomenon of manufacturers sneakily reducing the amount of product in their same-size packages, so as not to raise the price and anger customers. The report said consumers are noticing anyway. The 1937 version described it as follows: "Another crafty cheat, which extends to toilet articles and all sorts of human needs, is for the big controllers to steadily enlarge the package and make it flossier, to cover periodical reductions in net weight, but none in price. Even if the fixed price hasn't gone up, the net contents have been so subtly reduced that soon we're actually paying double the original price without noticing it."

Ice cream: *Consumer Reports* recently rated the most popular brands of ice creams and found many of them chock full of artificial ingredients. The authors of the 1937 book also begrudged the debasing of this most wonderful of desserts, referring scornfully to "drug store ice cream blown up with a bicycle pump."

Frugal Fashions

Chapter 2

HOW MANY HOURS A WEEK does the average Washingtonian work to pay for the clothes that he or she wears to work? It could be more than you realize.

According to a 1992 poll of 1,000 employed professional women done for *Working Woman* magazine, 62 percent of women said they spend between $100 to $300 for one work outfit. By contrast, only 23 percent said they spent less than $100, while 11 percent spent between $300 and $500, and 4 percent said they spent more than $500.

But resale shopping, judicious retail purchasing, and other frugal methods, such as borrowing, swapping, conserving, and yard saling, can cut the costs by two-thirds or more over traditional clothes buying. One can find plenty of attractive, serviceable clothing in Washington at very low cost.

According to a small sampling we conducted of local area clothing consignment shop owners in D.C., Maryland and Virginia, on the average purchase, the percentage of life, value or utility remaining in an item compared to its original, new and unused condition is 61 percent to 80 percent. Consignment shop owners told us that on average the percentage of savings they offered their customers compared to a local non-discount retail store was roughly 41 percent to 60 percent. The average purchase price of a woman's dress was $21 to $40; for a child's good dressy outfit it was $11 to $20.

Resale shop owners gave the following as examples of some of the best deals they sold in early 1996: a $3,000 Armani evening dress that sold for $250; a $1,800 fur coat for $800; a $350 crib for $125; a $4,000 full-length mink coat for $1,200; a $1,200 teak dining set for $225; and a $260 Hermes scarf for $80.

It's easy to seek high fashion without the high prices by knowing where to look. The following information is designed to help. These suggestions apply to men, women, and children. This chapter gives strategies for resale and off-price retail shopping. The rest of this chapter zeroes in on specific strategies for buying specialty types of clothing in Washington. As a comedian once said, "I started out as a child," so we will start at the very beginning, with the maternity wardrobe, with a side trip to buying a wedding dress, since the latter purchase can reach into the thousands of dollars.

This chapter also includes an extensive listing of consignment stores in Washington, and in suburban Maryland and northern Virginia, including their hours, and their policies for accepting consignments.

Tips for shopping resale

The following strategies can yield potential savings of thousands of dollars per year.

√ If you get to know the owner of a consignment shop, he or she might help you find specific items, i.e., call you when they come in. Ask to be remembered when your favorite designer, styles or sizes arrive. You can also consign your used clothing in good condition to cut your costs further. Most consignment stores offer a 50-50 split.

√ Visit frequently thrift and consignment shops that carry the type of clothing you're looking for, because there is a lot of turnover in these places.

√ Some consignment shops specialize in particular types of clothing, such as maternity or children's.

√ Don't shop as though you're in a retail store, where you expect to find clothes in your size and color whenever you go in. At secondhand places, don't think about what clothing is NOT there; look at what IS there. You might be looking for a skirt but instead find a beautiful blouse you can use. If it "calls out to you," get it because it might not be there tomorrow.

√ Keep a notebook listing the things you need—especially if you are shopping for a family. Record sizes and measurements for each family member. Measurements are more important because used clothing might not have the tag anymore that indicates size, and clothes may shrink through multiple washings. Take a tape measure with you when you shop.

√ Check out all the sizes, not just the sizes you usually wear. Different manufacturers cut their apparel differently; some clothes may have been altered. Whenever possible, try on clothes before buying. In stores with no dressing room, consider wearing solid color tights and leotard under your street clothes, so you can try on items in the store's selling area.

√ Examine all clothing carefully for defects. Don't be put off by small flaws. If an item is cheap enough, it might be worthwhile to stitch a seam, buy new buttons if a button or buttons are missing, or try to get a stain out.

√ Especially at yard sales, where items are often under a dollar, it is worth it to take the chance on a stained item. The following formula (developed by the owner of a second-hand children's clothing store) is excellent at getting out old stains: Put equal amounts of Cascade and Clorox 2 (or equivalent house brands, but not chlorine bleach) in a bucket (or the bathtub, depending on the size of the garment). Then fill the receptacle with the hottest water from the faucet and let the garment sit overnight in this mixture. Then wring out the garment and wash it as you would normally. Sometimes the process has to be repeated once or twice, but this gets out most stains.

√ As one is often told when purchasing new clothes, "buy classic styles" that you can wear year after year. Classic styles work very well in Washington, where power-suiting is more in vogue than anything in the pages of *Vogue* magazine. Know what colors and styles look good on you. Learn the signs of quality clothing. Learn which brand names hold up well (a designer label is no guarantee of this).

√ There may be some things you can't find

used. Buy used when you can; fill in with new items.

Take the bus to Potomac Mills

One grouping of retail stores in our geographical area is especially worth mentioning. Potomac Mills, the outlet mall with 220-plus stores in Dale City, Va., has a shuttle service available from D.C.-area metro stops. A friend who does not drive a car told us she has enjoyed several trips to the mall this way, and sees it as a real bargain.

The rates for the Potomac Mills bus are: $10 round trip, and $8 one way. Children under six ride free. Senior citizens age 62 and over are halfprice weekdays. Mondays and Tuesdays are reserved for groups of 10 people or more. The group rates are as follows: the group sponsor rides free; everyone else gets a free Potomac Mills shopping bag and a book of coupons worth about $250. A 20 percent discount on the fare is given for larger groups of at least 25 people.

To make reservations, call 703-551-1050 (this is a toll call from Washington). For information about Potomac Mills, contact the mall at (800) VAMILLS.

The trip takes roughly 45 minutes from Metro Center, depending on the number of passengers embarking. Other departure points in the past included Rosslyn Metro, Crystal City Metro, and Pentagon City Metro. Departures are as follows: Wednesday, Thursday and Friday, Dupont Circle red line metro Q St. exit 11:15 a.m.; 11:30 a.m. metro center 13th & G Sts N.W.; 11:45 a.m. Rosslyn metro; noon at Crystal City Gateway hotel; 12:15 Pentagon City. Departures from the mall occur at 5 p.m.

While the mall experience tends to foster higher prices and the likelihood of impulse buying, a well-planned jaunt, with list in hand, to retail discounters is often "worth it," and can yield a successful, yet frugal, shopping spree. A brochure put out by Potomac Mills offers these tips for frugal shopping:

√ dress comfortably;

√ prepare to shop by studying the layout of the massive mall for the stores you want to visit;

√ buy bargains when you find them rather than waiting, since an item may be gone later;

√ stock up on bargain gift items for future giving; and

√ take a break when needed.

The huge collection of stores is anchored by retailers J.C. Penney's, Spiegel, Marshalls, IKEA, Burlington Coat Factory, Waccamaw Pottery, and Nordstrom Rack Discount outlet. "Factory outlet" prices are also touted at stores such as Saks Fifth Avenue. Generally, store specialties include clothing, home furnishings, shoes, sports/fitness, jewelry, and fashion accessories.

Falling for consigning

When seasons change—when summer and winter enter their final phases—are the best times for D.C.-area frugalists to clean out their closets of clothing that they have outgrown (sizewise, stylewise, or otherwise) and to prepare the garments for consignment to local shops. Reselling your clothes is one way to further reduce costs. You will also become familiar with local shops and perhaps find a few that you will want to frequent for your own fashion needs.

Area consignment shop owners we interviewed told us that September is a big month for shopping, what with back-to-school, back-from-the-beach, backs-to-the-wheel and back-to-work on everyone's mind. Therefore, August is a good time to get clothes clean and ready to bring into the stores, some of which will begin accepting fall merchandise only after Labor Day. For the most part, at that time of the year summer items are not being taken on consignment. Similarly, March is a good time of year to bring in clothes for spring shopping.

What follows is a lengthy (although we do not claim it to be all-inclusive) list of area consignment stores in D.C., Maryland, and Virginia. Each listing includes the store's address, phone number, hours, and a brief synopsis of its consignment policies. It is always a good idea to call first before visiting because hours, policies, and even locations may change. Many stores specialize in women's clothing, several are limited to children's things and maternity, and a few are edging into antique store territory and take no clothing.

We hope readers will find an outlet (no pun intended) for some of their now-irrelevant items here. Area codes for phone numbers listed are 202 for D.C., 301 for Maryland, and 703 for Virginia. We have grouped the stores by geographic location for convenience. A listing here implies no endorsement by the editors.

Experience has taught us to open consignment accounts only at places we can get to conveniently to drop off and pick up. Remember to keep track of a store's hold policy. For example, if a shop only holds an item for 90 days before it becomes their property, make note of this. Also, some stores only accept consignments during workweek, daytime hours.

The rule-of-thumb these days for pricing an item for sale seems to be about one-third of the original retail price (our small sampling of store owners showed it to be slightly more than one-third). While many consignment stores used to price at one-half retail, as one store manager told us, there are "a lot of discount stores out there," so the consignment shops have to price even lower now to compete with them.

Herewith are the listings.

WASHINGTON, D.C.

- Clothes Encounters of a Second Kind. Women's clothing. 202 7th St. S.E.; 546-4004; 11-6 Mon-Fri, except open til 7 on Thurs; Sat 10-6; Sun 12-4. 50/50 split for consignors. Items must be recent fashions, in season, cleaned and pressed. They keep items two months; prices can be reduced after 30 days by 20-30%. Average price is 1/3 retail.

- Designer Too. Women's designer clothing. 3404 Connecticut Ave. N.W.; 686-6303. Mon-Sat 11-6; Sun 12-5. Consignments by appointment. Clothes must be dry-cleaned, on hangers, no older than two years. Usual pricing is one-third retail. 50/50 split. After one month, they mark down by 20%. Chanel sells "extremely well," also Armani, Ungaro, and Donna Karan.

- Once is Not Enough. Designer clothing for men and women; mostly upscale ladies clothing. 4830 MacArthur Blvd. N.W.; 337-3072. Mon-Sat 10-5. 50/50 split. Seasonal merchandise, they keep for 2 months. Clothes must be "mint condition," no more than 2 years old, on hangers. First consignment by appointment, minimum of six items first time. High-end designers such as Chanel and Armani. "Lowest" designer level they accept is Hugo Boss for men, Liz Claiborne for women, store manager tells us.
- The Pinnacle. Upscale designer women's clothing. 4932 Wisconsin Ave. N.W. 244-6300. 11-6 Mon-Sat. 50/50 split. Take consignments Mon, Wed, & Fri 11-6. No more than 30 items at a time. Must be cleaned & pressed, not necessarily on hangers. No synthetics, some blends allowed. They keep on seasonal basis, for 90 days; then items are donated or you pick up.
- Second Affair. Women's upscale clothing. 1904 18th St., N.W. 265-1829. 11:30-7:30 Tues-Fri., 10:30-5 Sat, 12-5 Sun, Closed Mon. Consignor gets 40 percent. Call for appointment to consign. All types of women's clothing accepted, including designer evening wear; must be clean. Clothes are kept for 60 days.
- Secondhand Rose of Georgetown. Women's designer clothes, furs, and accessories.

1516 Wisconsin Ave. N.W., 337-3378. 11-6 Mon.-Fri., 10-6 p.m. Sat. Minimum consignment each time of 8-10 items; items can be no more than two years old. Two-month contract, 50/50 split. Clothes accepted Mon-Fri 12:30-3:30. Need appointment to consign on Saturday.

* Secondi. Designer clothing for women. 1702 Connecticut Ave., N.W. 2nd floor. 667-1122. 11-6 Mon.-Sat., 1-5 Sunday, except in summer; hours extended in busier months. Everything from Chanel to the Gap, but their most popular designers are Ann Taylor, Donna Karan, Coach, and Anne Klein. Accept designer clothing no older than two years; it must be in fashion, in perfect condition, and in season. Consignments accepted by appointment Mon-Sat. 50/50 split.

* Status Two. 3023 M St., N.W.; 333-5454. Mon.-Sat. 11-6 p.m.; policy unavailable at presstime.

MARYLAND

* Almost New, 353 Muddy Branch Rd., Gaithersburg; 840-1013; 10-6 Mon-Wed; 10-8 Thurs; 10-7 Fri and Sat; 12-5 Sunday. 50-50 split for items that sell for more than $20; 40 percent to consignors for items that sell for under $20; the store keeps items 60 days; if they don't sell, they are given to charity. Items can be brought in Tues 10-1; Weds. 12-4.

* Carousel Consignments. Women's designer clothing, accessories, & jewelry. 12168 Nebel St., Rockville; 230-1300. Mon-Sat 10-6. 50/50 split. Items must be current styles; drycleaned & on

hangers. Minimum of eight items for first consignment. Appointment needed to consign; one-time $5 fee charged to consignors.

- Classic Consignment. Women's and children's clothing, accessories, jewelry. 2255 Bel Pre Rd., Silver Spring; 871-8522. Mon-Thurs 10-5, Fri 10-7, Sat 10-5, Sun 12-4.. 50/50 split. Items must be clean. Minimum of 20 non-clothing items per consignment. No appointment needed to consign Sun-Thurs. Annual $2 fee charged to consignors.
- Glad Rags. 7306 Carroll Ave., Takoma Park; 891-6870. Open 10-6, Mon-Sat; 12-4 Sun. Women's clothing vintage to modern. 50/50 split. Some men's and unisex clothing.
- Good Afternoon Consignment Shop (formerly Hanna's Consignment Shop), 6836 New Hampshire Ave., Takoma Park; 270-6106. Mon-Fri 12-7; Sat 10-7. 50/50 split. Consign items Mon-Thurs 12-4; in season, cleaned, pressed and on hangers. Takes shoes and handbags.
- Knee-High To A Grasshopper. Children's items (toys, furniture, as well as clothes infants to size 16). 7326 Carroll Ave., Takoma Park; 891-3124. Open 10-6 Mon-Sat ;12-4 Sun. 50/50 split. Items are kept for 90 days or a season. No hangers; they have their own & like the uniformity that provides. Items accepted any time.
- Marian's Connections. New and pre-owned clothing and accessories for women and children, prom dresses. 11221 Rose Lane, Wheaton; 942-5818. Open 11-5 Fri-Sat ;1-5 Sun. 50/50 split. Items accepted by appointment only.

- Seconds Unlimited, 4905 Allentown Rd., Camp Springs; 736-1030. 10-7 Mon, Tues, Thurs, Fri; Wed and Sat 10-6; closed Sun. 40% to consignor. Clothes priced at 1/3 to 1/2 original retail, depending on condition. Must be cleaned, pressed, and on hangers. Need to make appointment first time; not necessary after that. $5 per year consignment fee.
- The Ritz. 4847 Cordell Ave., Bethesda; 656-2330. Open 10-5 Mon-Sat. Women's designer apparel, career clothing, plus sizes, furs, designer purses, and accessories. No appointment necessary.
- Think-New Consignment Shop. 4912 Cordell Ave., Bethesda; 654-3313. Open 10-5 Mon-Sat. Men, women and children's clothing. 50/50 split. They send consignor copy of prices charged; items kept for a season. Clothes must be clean, ready to sell. Don't have to be on hangers.
- The Whole Kaboodle. Women's and children's clothing, including maternity wear and baby equipment. 16801 Crabbs Branch Way, Rockville; 670-0766. Mon.-Sat. 10-5:30 p.m., Thurs. til 8 p.m., closed Sun. Offers a selection of maternity clothing, has several racks of better larger sized clothes. 50/50 split; $5 annual fee. Accepts women's clothing on hangers, newly washed or dry-cleaned. Keeps clothes two months. No clothes older than two years.

VIRGINIA

- Classy Consignments. Clothing, shoes, jewelry, formal wear, baby items, housewares. 7100

Brookfield Plaza, Springfield; 644-4655. Mon-Fri 10-7; Sat 10-5; closed Sun Consignments by appointment only. 50/50 split. $8 annual consignment fee. Items stay for 65 days. Baby items "sell real well," manager says. Consignors work with consignees to set prices.

- Consigning Women. Clothing for women Sizes 2 to 3X; antiques. 6651-C Backlick Rd., Springfield; 569-2054. Mon-Wed 10-6; Thurs-Sat 10-8; Sun 12-5. Consignments by appointment only. 50/50 split; 90-day contract. 50 cents handling fee per item. Clothes must be "in saleable condition on hangers."
- EC's Closet. Designer clothing for women, career, evening, and plus sizes, crafts. 9415A Old Burke Lake Rd., Burke; 503-0772. Tues-Fri 11-6, Sat 10-4. Consignments by appointment only.
- New to You. Women's fine clothing and accessories. 125 N. Washington St., Falls Church; 533-1251; Tues-Sat 10-5. No appointment necessary during weekdays; consignments accepted by appointment on Saturdays. 50/50 split. Designer and better labels, no more than two years old. Vintage clothes 1950s and older. No lint, pet hairs, stains, or smoke odors. Prefer natural fibers.
- Odessa's Daughters. 10412 Main St. (upstairs), Fairfax; 359-8240. Tues-Sat 10-6. Contemporary from formal to casual, better vintage from the early 1900s, and retro vintage from the 1960s and 1970s, antique and contemporary jewelry and accessories.
- Once Cherished. Women's clothing, jew-

elry, collectibles. 141-4A Spring St., Herndon; 435-5141. Hours are Tues-Fri 11-6, Wed 11-7, Sat 11-5. Consignors 50/50; crafters get 65 percent of selling price. Up to 15 items (clean, excellent condition) per consignment. 60-day consignment period; unclaimed items are donated.

- Once Is Not Enough. Contemporary clothing and accessories. 428 N. Columbus St., Alexandria; 549-1129. 50/50 split. They hold items for two months; consignor paid at end of this time period. Must be on hangers, cleaned and pressed. No animal hair, odor-free, no smoke odors. $1 fee each time you consign. Maximum of 20 items per consignment.

- Quality Consignments Plus. Men's, women's, children's clothing/accessories, baby furnishings and toys, linens and decorator items. 3220 Old Pickett Rd., Fairfax; 591-8384. Mon, Tue, Wed, Fri 10-6; Thurs 10-7; Sat 10-5. Consign by appointment. Seasonal merchandise. 50/50 split. $5 annual fee; two-month contract; consignor paid at end of two months. They reduce items by 20% after one month; after two months, marked down 30%..

- Second Childhood. Children's and maternity. 2647 N. Pershing Drive, Arlington; 276-7740. Hours Tue-Sat. 11-6; Thurs 11-7. 50/50 split.

- Shirley's Consignments. See Appendix for sample policy. 14834 Build America Dr., Woodbridge; 491-6159. Mon., Weds., Fri., Sat. 10-5; Tues., Thurs. 10-7.

- Second Glance. Women's clothing & accessories. 821 King St. Alexandria; 836-0737.

Tues.-Sat. 8-6 p.m. 50/50 split; 3-month contract. Minimum number of 5 items. Clothes must be cleaned; don't have to be drycleaned because manager says "drycleaning is expensive." She'd rather look at an item, then maybe say, "I'll take it if you get it drycleaned."

• Twice upon a Child. Clothing, toys, furniture, books, maternity wear, handmade crafts. 32 Pidgeon Hill Drive, Sterling; 406-0601. Tues., Weds., Fri. 10-6:30, Thurs. 10-8, Sat. 10-4:30. 50/50 split. $7.50 fee per year. Need appointment to consign. No more than 40 items at a time. Sizes newborn to 16. Clothing held for 90 days, then is donated or consignor can reclaim.

Twice-a-year-sales

Dani's Duds is the Brigadoon of area consignment sales. Like the Scottish town in the Lerner and Loewe musical that appears only once every 100 years, the Dani's Duds children's consignment sale is conducted twice a year (the sale runs for two weekends each time) at a large rented store facility in Northern Virginia. A wide range of items

---

More signs of the frugal times . . .

"What's old is new again..."

(From a 1995 newspaper ad for the very tony, upscale retail department store Nordstrom. The store was offering what it called "The best of men's and women's recycled clothing." The company's ad said, "everything in mint condition, just like the original—except the price tag." Frugalists, however, may shudder at suggested prices of $24 for wool blazers, $26 for jeans, and $18 for vests or corduroy shirts. Located at malls in Tysons, Montgomery, Towson, Annapolis.)

are made available and items are further discounted during the latter part of the sale. She also is beginning a twice-a-year sale for women.

Dani's Duds also publishes a free, bimonthly newspaper, also called Dani's Duds, whose articles concentrate on topics of interest to families. To get on the mailing list for the newspaper or to get information on how to consign, call (703) 716-9797, or write P.O. Box 503, Merrifield, VA 22116.

The city of Bowie, Maryland also conducts a twice-a-year secondhand children's items sale, called the Children's Trading Post. The sale is conducted once in the fall and once in the spring, also over a two-day period each time, and is held at a public facility such as the city park ice arena or the local high school. Unlike the Dani's Duds sale, for which items are taken on consignment, people with items to sell for the trading post may purchase a space from the city. For information, call Bowie City Hall at (301) 262-6200.

A hint for cleaning clothes

Here's a hint for cleaning fine washables. We noticed that the blurb on the back of Sunlight dish liquid includes a terse line: "great for fine washables too." That's it: "great." It didn't say how much to use, or how to use it. Since Sunlight is much cheaper than Woolite, the standard bottled product for fine washables, we decided to call Lever Brothers, manufacturer of Sunlight.

After we ascertained that Woolite is not a Lever Brothers product, the customer service representative said that "yes, it is a recommended use," for both Sunlight and Dove dish washing liquid. He advised to add a tablespoonful, a capful, or a squirt to a gallon of water and to wash by hand. Don't use in the washing machine, though, because it oversuds. A quick inventory at the grocery store showed that many different brands of dishwasher detergent advised that the product could be used this way.

Wedding gown radiance (without extravagance)

Remember that scene in *Gone With the Wind* where Scarlett O'Hara swoops down the stairs in a lovely forest-green velvet gown she made of material that formerly draped one of the high, graceful windows of Tara?

Only her workworn hands gave her secret away. Of course when Carol Burnett parodied this scene many years later, she left the drapery hardware in the dress, which made it a little more obvious ...

Assuming a modern bride-to-be does not do something like Carol did, however, she can buy (or rent) a beautiful wedding dress for a fraction of retail cost, and no one has to be aware (unless she doesn't care if people know what a sensible wife her future husband is getting).

The prices of wedding gowns have climbed astronomically in recent years, to the point where it is now commonplace for these dresses to cost thousands of dollars. Forty years ago you could buy a small house for what a designer wedding dress now costs! We believe these prices to be out of line and out of step with the current, increasingly frugal times.

Like the car that runs fine on inexpensive regular gas whose owner insists on feeding it premium because "it must be the best because it costs the most," some brides seem to think that a more expensive dress makes them more married. It doesn't—it's the license, which usually costs under $10, that achieves that goal.

If a bride spends, for example, $500 for a previously owned gown instead of $2,000 for a brand-new one (remember, these have usually been worn just once for four or five hours) that's $1,500 that can be put towards a dreamier honeymoon, a start on a home down payment, or a state-of-the-art stereo system for the love nest! And she'll look just as radiant!

Here are a few of the places and methods you can use to save hundreds of dollars on a wedding dress and still look radiant on the big day:

WANT ADS—Sad to say, sometimes women buy their dream wedding dress, get it fitted and altered, and then discover they will not be getting married after all. You can often find ads in the local newspapers advertising "designer gown never worn," or "cost $3,000, will sacrifice for $500."

It's easy to understand why someone would want to get rid of the dress, but don't be superstitious—it's just cloth and it might be exactly what you're looking for, or would be with just a few alterations.

BRIDAL CONSIGNMENT SHOPS—there

are several shops in the area that specialize in secondhand wedding gowns; most of these dresses are just a few years old. Most see customers only by appointment. Among these are: "I Do, I Do" in Rockville, Md. (301) 762-4464; with about 500 gowns, the average price of a dress is $400 to $800, some designer items are higher, less formal gowns run about $100-$350; also available: headpieces, shoes, purses, and bridal hose.

"Something Old, Something New" in Laurel, Md. (301) 490-6642, offers about 350 dresses, sizes 2-24, most gowns in the $400-$500 range, some less; it also sells headpieces, some bridesmaid dresses ($75 to $90 range), some shoes (if you can find your size, most of these are $10), and a few flower girl dresses.

BRIDAL DEPARTMENTS IN WIDER-RANGING CONSIGNMENT SHOPS—One consignment store owner told us that 75 percent of her gowns were obtained brand-new from bridal shops that closed or from people who did not get married. She had some vintage dresses from the 1940s and even earlier. She noted that some brides will buy a vintage dress "in fair condition" at a low price, spend $200 to $300 to have a seamstress renovate it, and have a unique wedding gown.

One can get very creative with wedding gowns. This shop owner noted that it has not always been de rigueur for brides to wear white, pointing out a number of champagne-colored or pink vintage wedding gowns. She even showed us a picture of a rather grim-faced 19th-century bride wearing a black wedding gown...

DAVID'S BRIDAL SUPERSTORE—This outlet for new wedding gowns, opened January 1993 as part of an East Coast chain. Most gowns have the labels removed; price range is $199 to $1,499. Also here you can find veils, mother of bride dresses, bridesmaid and flower girl dresses. Gowns can be purchased off the rack. A seamstress is employed on the premises; (703) 912-7701; 7269 Commerce St., Springfield, Va. Open M-F 11 a.m. to 9 p.m., Sat 10 a.m. to 6 p.m., Sunday 11 a.m. to 5 p.m. Another location opened even more recently, is 11550-A Rockville Pike, Rockville, Md., (301) 881-1112.

Headpieces can get quite expensive if they are purchased new, but these costs also can be avoided with some creativity. One person we know had a headpiece made of silk flowers in the colors of her wedding at Ben Franklin craft stores—it contained "pearls," and small white, burgundy, and mauve silk roses. The cost was $12. Look in consignment and thrift stores and then make your own if you're "sew" inclined.

FORMAL WEAR OUTLETS—Previously rented gowns can be purchased at formal wear establishments such as Masters Tuxedo, which has stores in Gaithersburg, Forestville, and Falls Church. Tuxedos are available too, and the guys usually get more wear out of these than the women do with their gowns. The entire wedding party can rent their attire too, which brings us to ...

BRIDAL RENTALS—The Heirloom Collection in Olney, Md., for $285 (four-day rental) will rent a bridal outfit that includes a gown with a train, headpiece, veil, and crinoline, sizes 4 to 24. The gowns would retail for $1,000 or more; (301) 924-2908. Young's Bridal Rental in Fairfax, Va. (703) 352-5649 offers for rent new dresses, at a cost of $300-$500; shoes, headpieces, crinolines, and other items also are available. Some vintage gowns from the 1940s and 1950s can also be found here.

INHERIT A DRESS—Maybe you CAN wear your mother's dress, perhaps with some alterations, a little updating, etc. It does give one pause when one sees modern brides spend thousands of dollars for a dress, then fork out a few hundred dollars more to get a dry cleaner to "heirloom preserve" it, presumably for their daughter(s)? Is this a hint to as-yet-unborn progeny not to spend thousands of dollars on a NEW wedding dress even if their mothers did?

We're not sure there's a logical connection here ... Another note: consignment stores are also good sources of prom dresses, which apparently nowadays kind of resemble cocktail dresses of the 1950s and can cost up to $500 at a formal store, according to a teen we interviewed.

To summarize, when it comes to The Wedding Dress, as someone noted in another equally weighty context: Stop the Insanity! A dress need not cost the same as the furnishings in your first apartment!

Mustering a maternity wardrobe

Finding clothes to suit the pregnant woman, with her ever-changing figure, can be an expensive venture, especially in the Washington, D.C. area, with its large numbers of working women who must look professional day after day. But many women refuse to pay hundreds of dollars for a wardrobe that will be used for only six to nine months, depending on an individual's weight gain and the time it takes after pregnancy to regain one's shape. They would prefer instead to use their money toward items for the baby.

With so many options for building a maternity wardrobe, women can find a happy, frugal medium for their personal budget that begins with garage sale finds and stops short of full-price, retail maternity store styles.

Planning ahead will help stave off overspending. One way is to set a budget and determine the clothing basics that you will need to get you through the months ahead, regardless of the season. These may include: a pair of jeans; one or two pairs of knit slacks; several tee-shirts and sweat shirts; two fancy dresses or other outfits for social occasions (more, if you go out or entertain a lot— these can also be rented); several pairs of low-heeled shoes; a cardigan to fend off a winter chill or an air-conditioned one. Shorts in summer and turtlenecks in winter are other, standard must-haves.

Going one step further, an analysis of the seasons and your personal work and play needs will yield a good guess of the minimum amount of clothing that will get you by. For instance, if you work in an office five days per week, you probably will need at least five work outfits. Since those outfits must fit you when you are at six months and at nine months, you could double that number to 10 to obtain a conservative estimate. Also, if you exercise, participate in a sport, or other activity such as a choir, where you need a uniform of sorts, be sure to consider those purchases in your budget.

If you anticipate a special occasion, such as a wedding, will occur sometime in the course of your pregnancy, you can estimate your size and start looking for a rental outfit or a secondhand find. But for a daily wardrobe, the best places for maternity clothes are as follows, in order of preference for saving money.

Friends, family, or co-workers. These helpful persons will often loan or give you clothing. Thank your lucky stars if you are fortunate enough to start a wardrobe at this point. Often the people you know who have recently been pregnant are either the wrong size; had their babies during a different season than you (for example, they were heavier in the summer, and you will be heavier in the winter); or have already gotten rid of their wardrobes (since many women can't wait to get into regular clothes again).

Yard sales. By using yard sale finds as the foundation of your wardrobe, (such as a basic navy blue knit dress with gold buttons for $3), you can fill in and accessorize with items bought at retail or consignment stores, if necessary, to develop a truly professional appearance or simply a spiffy look.

Thrift shops. Thrift shops run for the benefit of churches, hospitals and other charities are always sources of real bargain basement finds. While such places require somewhat more shopping effort, since you usually have to comb through boxes of unsorted items, they have the added advantage of contributing needed funds to worthwhile organizations. One person we know found a rayon print maternity top for spring from Saks Fifth Avenue at such a shop for a mere seventy-five cents. A knit jumpsuit with stirrups from a prominent local maternity store was also found for $2. Both were in perfect condition.

Consignment stores. Building a wardrobe from consigned articles is easier than hunting at yard sales and thrift shops. In this venue, you can realistically expect to find key items in your size and season, especially if you visit one, two or three shops fairly regularly. As with all consignment shopping, the more often she visits, the more likely the pregnant woman is to find items she likes and that fit. However, such visits need not take a lot of time, particularly when you are familiar with the stores and have in mind the items you want.

Several consignment shops in the area are devoted to maternity clothes along with infant's and children's clothes and accoutrements such as furniture, car seats, baby swings, etc. Moms-to-be will find the range of other items especially useful toward the end of pregnancy when they start to seriously focus on outfitting their new arrivals. They are also great sources to return to when you and baby have outgrown earlier finds and it is time for you to be the consignor..

Larger Size Womens' Clothing Stores. Both the off-price and retail versions of these stores, such as Lane Bryant and other "plus-size" chains, have a wide selection of items and offer sales and clearances of non-seasonal merchandise (perfect for the pregnant woman who foresees larger-sized times.)

Retail Outlet Stores and Discount Department Stores. Very reasonable prices can be had here if you stick with sale items at retail outlets, and shop carefully at the discount houses, like K-Mart, avoiding lower quality "loss leader" merchandise. So-called maternity factory outlet stores should be shopped cautiously.

Department Stores. Montgomery Ward, Sears, and J.C. Penney are among the few department stores that still carry a maternity line. Though the pickings are slim even at these behemoth merchandisers, these stores offer value-priced basics from dresses to nursing nighties.

Specialty Maternity Stores. Once you get past the sticker shock here, you might want to consider purchasing just one special, high quality outfit or item to fill in your frugal wardrobe.

Five easy tips for yard sale shopping success

Some of the cheapest (and highest quality) clothing around can be picked up at yard sales. We therefore offer the following tips to make the most out of your yard sale forays.

√ If you're a Saturday morning yard-saler,

map out your strategy by going through the garage/yard sale ads in local papers early in the week, as soon as the paper comes out, if possible. Look up the street on your map. Take the map with you.

√ Figure out which advertised sales seem promising for you by keeping a general list of things you need or want.

√ Moving sales often yield a wider range of merchandise than "clean out your closet" type sales. Moving sales may also have higher prices. Community-wide yard sales, where several neighbors in one area hold their sales on the same day, by far are the best for saving time. These events enable you to go to many sales in one central location.

√ Get up early so you can have first pick, but note arriving extremely early can be unsettling and annoying for sellers.

√ Bring one-dollar bills and quarters for easier buying and (if it is your style) bargaining. *Happy hunting!*

Home Frugal Home

Chapter 3

SAVING MONEY AROUND THE HOME does not only mean "do it yourself." Although that is a key frugal tactic for keeping down all kinds of home maintenance costs, there are many ways unhandy frugalists can save, too.

One of the best is to lower the cost of items purchased for use in your home by using the price matching policies offered by area retail stores.

The way price matching usually works is this: customers who find a lower price on the same item at a different store can obtain a certain percentage, typically 10 percent, off the price of an item. These items can range from dishwashers and answering machines to perfume and turkeys. But watch out, because the fine print varies from store to store.

A friend of ours decided to put new, white mini-blinds on all the windows in her house, to replace old and tattered shades. She went to Hechinger's, hoping to pick up just two (to see how they would look). She found them and paid about $25 each.

The next weekend, Home Depot advertised in the Sunday circular the identical item for about half that price. When she arrived, however, the store was out of stock of the particular size she needed. A store clerk advised her that additional stock would arrive within a week to 10 days. Not wanting to wait, she traipsed over to Hechinger. Voila, they had plenty in stock! But (gasp!) they still cost almost twice what the item did at Home Depot.

As she wandered Hechinger's aisles pondering this frugalist's dilemma, she noticed signs saying the store would match any competitor's advertised price, and reduce the final price an additional 10 percent. Pulling the Home Depot ad out of her purse, she went to the cashier with 14 mini-blinds in her cart. The cashier acted a bit flustered at first, and called the manager over. That person accurately took down the price and was just getting ready to enter it into the cash register, when the customer reminded him of the store's posted policy of reducing the price by another 10 percent. He did not balk at the notion, but he did have to rewrite the initial calculations again on a form before entering the price into the cash register.

The whole transaction took about 15 minutes longer than if the customer had just paid the full amount. But in 15 minutes time, she saved herself roughly $151.80. The calculations were as follows: Original price: 10 mini-blinds x $25 = $250, plus 4 mini-blinds x $17 = $68 (a different size) for a total of $318. Price-matched price: 10 mini-blinds x $12.62 = $126.20, plus 4 mini-blinds x $10 = $40, for a total of $166.20. The difference: $318 - $166.20=$151.80.

That 15 minutes worth of work, completed at an hourly rate would be an hourly wage of $607.20! So the extra 15 minutes was well worth it to this customer. As an old English proverb states, "Fru-

> **TIPS FOR USING PRICE MATCHING POLICIES**
> ☑ **Find** advertised price matching policy and read fine print carefully.
> ☑ **Look** for 10 percent discount off the item itself, not 10 percent of the difference.
> ☑ **Find** out how long the price guarantee is honored: 14 days, 30 days, 1 year, or what.
> ☑ **Make** sure model numbers match before asking for a discount, or, get a fact sheet on the product to compare features.
> ☑ **Make** phone calls when possible to quickly get price quotes.
> ☑ **Ask** for discounts, or negotiate price matches if a policy is not posted or found through an ad.

gality is an income." By the way, she later brought her receipt back for the original two mini-blinds and Hechinger reimbursed her for the difference between its price and the Home Depot price.

In another case of price matching, Home Depot said it would lower the price of an in-stock Whirlpool electric oven, if the customer simply found the exact model elsewhere for less. This particular customer, with a couple of phone calls, was easily able to locate a retailer who was selling the oven for just $20 less. But that $20 was parlayed into about $92 because Home Depot then sold the oven to the customer at the lower price and took off another 10 percent, which on a $720 item, was $72. The other retailer's price was not advertised, but Home Depot confirmed it with a phone call of its own.

Price matching pros and cons

Using a store's price matching policy is sometimes trying for several reasons. Some price matching policies are limited to

14 days or 30 days, depending on the store. Some stores do not specify.

Matching models is not as easy as matching prices and this is one way retailers protect themselves from losing profits on items such as bedding and mattresses, televisions, videotape recorders.

While the customer should never expect to get something for nothing, it is reasonable to expect that when model numbers differ at two stores, but the key features of an item are the same, some discount should be given. Although a company is not required to honor a price matching policy in this kind of circumstance, the customer has the opportunity for negotiation, according to one source, a former salesman with 10 years' experience in video retail sales. Some stores will do this, some will not. Department stores long have had different model numbers made specifically for them, the former salesman said. A customer is free to go buy the item elsewhere and the company won't make any profit at all if that happens, so it is worth it for both parties to work something out.

Price matching is a good negotiating tool for the frugal consumer. While a manager may not match a price on a lawn mower, for example, he or she may modify the price downward to make it worthwhile to the consumer to purchase it at his/her store. This is a good, old-fashioned way of doing business, according to the former salesman. Good managers of stores large and small want to keep good customers satisfied, and customers want to deal with a vendor they can trust. And it's always possible that if consumers fail to use the policies, retailers will simply stop offering them.

The former salesman suggested that consumers make phone calls when possible to quickly get price quotes for comparisons, and that they call on weekdays, rather than weekends, when business tends to be slower and clerks are more inclined to be helpful.

But on big-ticket items, stores generally want to verify a price, if not through an ad, then at least through a phone call. If you can get the price over the phone, then chances are, the store can too, especially if you provide the store's phone number and the person with whom you spoke.

It is also a good idea to research items through other sources. For example, you might look up key features and model numbers in publications such as *Washington Consumers Checkbook* to obtain additional information on pricing and availability.

Different stores, policies

Policies vary by type of store. A hardware or home improvement retailer may include all inventory items in a store in the posted policy, while a department store may limit it to electrical appliances. So the only way to find out for sure is to check with the store itself.

Many people save dollars off the price of an item simply by asking for a reduction. Often their reasoning is that the item is going to go on sale within a few days, or some other retailer has it on sale, or it has a minor flaw, or the customer simply does not want to pay full price.

Some recent examples of price matching policies follow:

- Best Buy, a consumer electronics store with branches in Maryland and Virginia, advertises they will beat the competition's lowest price, if "within 30 days of your purchase from Best Buy, you find a competitor offering a lower price, we'll refund the difference plus another 10 percent of the difference." The policy does not apply to special, bonus or free offers.

- Home Depot advertises, "If you should ever find a lower price on an item we stock, even if it's an 'advertised special', we'll not only meet that price, we'll beat it by 10 percent for bringing it to our attention." (That's 10 percent on the price, not on the difference.)

- Hechinger has essentially the same policy as Home Depot, but its advertised plan specifies "if you see an identical stocked item priced less at any retail store or warehouse club, advertised or not, we'll thank you by taking 10 percent off the competitor's price. The only exceptions are clearance and closeout items."

- Department store mainstay Montgomery Ward says its price protection guarantee is as follows: they will match any store's current advertised price at time of merchandise purchase, plus if you find a lower advertised price at any store, including Montgomery Ward within 30 days after purchase, the store will "cheerfully refund the difference." On electrical appliances and auto items, the store boasts that it will also "refund 110 percent of the difference" and sometimes, during special events, 150 percent of the difference. (Remember, that's the difference between two prices, not the price itself, which results in a much higher number.)

• KMart has a so-called pricing policy. KMart states that advertised items are either their everyday price or a sale price (but they don't tell you which). Also, according to a company ad, "if an advertised item is not available for purchase due to any unforeseen reason, KMart will issue a rain check on request for the merchandise (one item or reasonable family quantity) to be purchased at the advertised price whenever available, or will sell you a comparable quality item at a comparable price."

Finding frugalist furniture

According to another yardsale gem of a book, the *Pocketbook Guide to Furniture Buying,* a 3-inch by 3-inch spiral bound booklet published in 1963 by furniture maker Kroehler Mfg. Co.:

"All the authorities today say the same: Trust your own instincts! It's your home and no one else's. It is vital that you please yourself and your family first. Don't ask for advice from Aunt Minnie, your bridge club or the milkman! Remember, they aren't going to live in your home."

Kroehler had a bias toward new furniture, since that is what the company sold. But Lynette Jennings, host of cable TV's *Homeworks* show, advocates buying furnishings used. She contends there's "something magical" about putting together a roomful of mismatched furniture that works.

"And it can be done on a budget," Jennings says. She advises her viewers to go for casual elegance in creating a formal living room, making it a place that people want to sit in and enjoy.

An inexpensive trick often recommended by decorating experts is to use wall paint to create a new or different look. Jennings suggests that painting the walls in a living room a dark color such as burgundy or forest green, lends a rich look. She says such walls make anything in the room look "much richer than it actually is."

The cost of paint can be as little as $5.99 a gallon on sale at Sears to $19.99 for Behr premium titanium at Home Depot. There are a range of prices in between at Lowe's, Montgomery Ward, KMart, Hechinger's, Duron, and other retail outlets. Hechinger's top brand, Martin Senour, for example, is made by Sherwin Williams, which charges more on average for its paint when sold at the Sherwin Williams store.

Jennings suggested for an elegant occasional table putting a silver tray atop a wooden luggage rack, such as one would find in hotel rooms. A consumer we know found just such a rack in dark cherry wood, with nary a scratch for a mere $12 at Secondhand Rose in Rockville, Md.

The shopping pyramid of prices

Some of these furniture treasures can be found at reasonable prices at the numerous consignment and thrift stores throughout our area. There is, of course, no substitute for the omnipresent garage sale to pick up strange and unusual items, like an old iron gate, or unique, leftover, drapery fabric.

As such, we present for future consideration as you peruse this volume, what we like to call The Shopping Pyramid of Prices. This is a general framework for thinking about the cost of an item, used and new, on the basis of where one purchases it. It applies to all types of consumer items from furniture and clothing to electronics, sporting goods, and cosmetics.

At places listed in the top part of the pyramid, one is likely to often find an item for the lowest price. Places at the bottom part of the pyramid generally yield higher prices. In between, there can be a range, from least to most expensive. But good deals can be found at all of these venues. In print, it might look something like this:

$

YARD SALES

FLEA MARKETS

MOVING, ESTATE SALES

AUCTIONS (can be exciting)

CLASSIFIED ADS (good for specific items)

THRIFT SHOPS (items donated, usually older)

CONSIGNMENT SHOPS (usually for profit)

SPECIALIZED SECONDHAND SHOPS

RETAIL STORES' WAREHOUSES; CLUBS

(GENUINE) FACTORY OUTLET STORES

SALES IN DISCOUNT CHAIN STORES

CATEGORY STORES (discount merchandise)

CATALOG STORES (discounted housewares)

SALES, CLEARANCES IN RETAIL STORES

$ $ $ $ FULL PRICE IN RETAIL STORE $ $ $$

Local resale furnishings stores

For regular household furniture, there are several resale places that have excellent turnover of merchandise, which generally means a good selection most of the time. We again remind you to call first before visiting these establishments if you want to confirm any particular information listed here, since stores can and do change hours, policies, and locations. For more ideas, see Chapter 7, Community Focus.

- AB's Consignments & Collectables. A lot of "smalls" — bric a bric, pictures. Some furniture. 3734 Howard Ave., Kensington, Md. (301) 946-9646. Hours are 10-6 Tues-Sat; 12-5 Sun. Bring in consignments on Tuesday from 10-4. New consignors can come in only once a month, the last Tuesday of the month. 50/50 split. They keep an item 90 days; then it's the consignor's responsibility to pick it up.

- Alexandria Upscale Resale. Furniture. 1456 Duke St., Alexandria; Va. 683-3333; Mon 10-8; Tues-Sat 10-6; Sun 12-5. 50/50 split for items they price under $1,000; 60% to consignor for items priced higher than that. Can consign Mon-Fri. They keep items for up to 90 days, but try to sell within 30 days; markdowns then are taken. Bring picture of large items so they can evaluate.

- Amaryllis Vintage Co. Inc. Upscale resales. 4922 Wisconsin Ave., N.W. Wash., D.C. (202) 224-2211.

- Amvets Thrift Stores. Furniture, televisions, bric-o-brac, clothing. Proceeds benefit programs for veterans. Locations at 6101 Georgia

Ave., N.W., Washington; 5944 Martin Luther King Blvd., Seat Pleasant, Md.; 7844 Richmond Highway, Alexandri, Va.; and 9880 Washington Blvd., Laurel, Md.

* Consignment Furniture Gallery at 11722 Nicholson Lane, Rockville, Md. (301) 770-4400. Hours are 10-6 Tues-Sat except Thurs 10-8:30, Sun 12-5.

* Cordell Collection, 4911 Cordell Ave., Bethesda, MD (301) 907-3324.5. Furniture. 4911 Cordell Ave., Bethesda, Md.; 907-3324. Mon-Sat 10-5. 50/50 split; keep items for 90 days. For large items, they like a picture & measurements first. With pre-approval, consignors can bring in large pieces Mon-Sat. Small things can be brought in (without pre-approval) Tues-Fri. Priced about 1/2 retail, depending on condition.

* Good After New. 9-6 Mon -Fri, 9-5 Sat; 4865 Cordell Ave., Bethesda, Md. (301) 907-3448.

* Goodwill Stores, throughout the area in Northeast D.C.; Bladensburg, District Heights, Gaithersburg, Langley Park, Md.; and Alexandria, Arlington, Falls Church, and Woodbridge, Va.

* Past & Present Shop, near Entenmann's in the Sunshine Square, at 1327 Rockville Pike, Rockville, Md. (301) 738-3961. Mon.-Fri. 9-7, Sat., Sun. 10-6.

* Second Hand Rose. Consignment and thrift store. Furniture, appliances, paintings, records, compact discs, tools, office supplies, clothing. 730 East Gude Dr., Rockville, Md. (301) 424-5524; Mon-Fri 10-6, Sat 10-4, Sun 1-5.

- The Upscale Resale Shop. A thrift shop carrying furniture, housewares, records, tapes, compact discs, books, jewelry, clothes. Owned and operated by Jobs Unlimited Inc., which provides vocational training for persons with mental illness. 1075 Rockville Pike, Rockville, Md. Mon-10-7; Sun 12-5.
- Upscale Resale. Can consign, without appointment seven days a week. 8100 Lee Hwy., Falls Church, Va.., Mon-Fri 10-9; 10-6 Sat; Sun 12-5. (703) 698-8100.
- Westover Thrift Shop, 5906 N. Washington Blvd, Arlington, Va. 10-6 Mon thru Sat. (703) 241-9227.

Not another lightbulb joke

The Potomac Electric Power Co. (PEPCO) in the past has given out coupons to defray the cost of expensive, but energy efficient light bulbs. The long-term savings of such bulbs outweigh the initial costs, according to PEPCO. The bulbs can save a customer 30 percent to 75 percent of the electricity now used to light a home. Lighting costs can represent up to 20 percent of a home's electric bill. Depending on usage, the bulbs may only need to be replaced once every five years.

In 1995, an environmental group working with that stalwart industry beacon the Edison Electric Institute launched an ad campaign, acknowledging that millions of the energy efficient light bulbs have been sold nationally, in part because the utility companies themselves have promoted the new

> **More signs of the frugal times**
>
> "Saving money is conservation at its most basic."
>
> (From a story in the July/August 1995 issue of *E, The Environmental Magazine*. The cover story, entitled "The Real Conservatives," says that in this age of abundance, the practice of reuse is making a comback. Even companies are getting into it, such as Xerox, which rebuilds some of its copiers and guarantees them like new products. Such "remanufacturing" is also showing up in auto parts and kitchen appliances. A used rubber company makes purses from old inner tubes.)

bulbs. But other utility companies in the D.C. area have yet to follow suit, so non-PEPCO customers will have to pay higher prices to ultimately lower their electric bills.

Retailers in D.C., Prince Georges and Montgomery Counties accepted the Pepco coupons. Customers received booklets with roughly $200 worth of coupons that could be applied to brands such as: General Electric, Sylvania, Philips, Panasonic, and Lights of America.

To properly replace your old bulbs with the newer ones, make a list of the lights you want to retrofit; for each lamp or fixture, write down the size, shape and wattage of the current bulb; then compare the height and width of the harp portion of your lamps with the dimensions of the new bulbs to see if you also need to purchase inexpensive harp or socket extenders.

A note about types of bulbs. The compact fluorescents are *not* suitable for fixtures with dimmers or unprotected outdoor fixtures, but the tungsten halogen bulbs *can* be used for these purposes.

PEPCO also reminds customers that a water heater can use more electricity than any other appliance in a home except the heating/air conditioning system. So, the energy company promotes the use of water saving shower heads, fiberglass water heater blankets, faucet aerators, and pipe insulation. If your water heater isn't insulated, much of the energy is escaping and forcing the heater to turn on more frequently, using more energy to heat the same water over again, PEPCO says.

Consumer contacts

The following is a listing of local consumer contacts. The groups issue information, provide advice, and generally offer assistance in a variety of areas, including product information, debt counseling, and local consumer complaints.

Because of budget cuts and administrative changes, numbers and offices have been known to change ocassionally, so call first.

- Alexandria, Va., Consumer Affairs, Box 178 City Hall, Alexandria, VA 22313 (703) 838-4350.
- Better Business Bureau of Metropolitan Washington, 1012

More signs of the frugal times . . .

"Like houses across America, the House of Representatives is having a yard sale Saturday." (From an article in the Sept. 21, 1995 *The Washington Times,* about the House's first foray into homespun frugality. The successful sale unloaded thousands of items, ranging from the Ways and Means Committee's 20-foot long oval mahogany table, to what some euphemistically called congressional memorabilia--old sofas, chairs, desks, filing cabinets, books, decorative items. Goal: to clear the warehouse where the items were stored at a cost of $235,000 a year.)

14th St. NW, Washington, DC 20005 (202) 393-8000.
• Consumer Credit Counseling Service of Greater Washington, Inc., 15847 Crabbs Branch Way, Rockville, MD 20855 (301) 590-1010. Free credit counseling.
• Consumer Federation of America, 1424 16th St. N.W. Suite 604, Washington, DC 20036, (202) 387-6121. Fax: (202) 265-7989.
• Consumers Union of the United States (Washington office) (202 462-6262, 1666 Connecticut Ave. N.W., Suite 310, Washington, DC 20009.
• Fairfax County Dept. of Consumer Affairs, 12000 Government Center Parkway, Suite 552, Fairfax VA 22035 (703) 324-4636, recorded info.
• Garden Resources of Washington (GROW), 1419 V St. N.W., Washington, DC 20009, (202) 234-0591, a non-profit organization that helps people start community food gardens.
• Maryland Attorney General's Consumer Protection Office, 200 St. Paul Place, 16th Floor, Baltimore, MD 21202, (301) 470-7534, or (410) 528-8662.
• Montgomery County Office of Consumer Affairs, 100 Maryland Ave., Rockville, MD 20850 (301) 217-7374.
• Prince George's County Office of Citizens & Consumer Affairs, County Administration Building, 14741 Oden Bowie Drive, Upper Marlboro, MD 20772-3050 (301) 952-3000.
• University of Maryland Cooperative Ex-

tension Service, 6707 Groveton Dr., Clinton, MD 20735, (301) 868-9410. Free credit counseling.

- U.S. Consumer Product Safety Commission hotline (for recall information on unsafe products and for consumers to provide such information) 1-800-638-2772.
- *Washington Consumers Checkbook*, 806 15th St. NW, Washington, DC 20005(202) 347-7283.

Mulch ado about gardening

Remember how Chauncey the gardener in the movie *Being There* seemed incredibly wise as he spoke in terms of gardening for nearly every situation he encountered, and conveyed, in effect, a metaphor for life? Well, gardening and frugality are similarly entwined.

Gardeners often seek to waste nearly nothing with their avocation, returning much of the earth's bounty to the soil from whence it came. Thanks to such frugal natures, they know a good bargain when they see one.

Knowledge is key to successful gardening. Twenty years ago, the first edition (1974) of *The Gardener's Catalogue* contained no ads, the authors said, because it was a catalogue of information, what they called "the most important tool since the watering can."

In the metro area, expert advice, information, and assistance on lawn and garden care can be obtained free from many governmental and commercial sources. State cooperative extension services through land grant universities run hotlines in local county offices that residents can call to have their technical questions answered. Locally, these are located at the University of Maryland, Virginia Polytechnic Institute, the University of Virginia, and the University of the District of Columbia.

• In Northern Virginia, the Fairfax County Department of Extension reccomends calling the National Pest Control Association for information on pesticides, (703) 573-8330. Also, for information on plant clinics conducted through the county's library system, call (703) 324-5393.

• For gardeners who want support from fellow enthusiasts, a good place to start is the National Arboretum. Part of the U.S. Department of Agriculture, it is located at 3501 New York Ave., N.E., (202) 245-2726. While it does not have a hotline, it maintains nine miles of gardens in Northeast Washington, which can be visited free, and it is the unofficial headquarters of the National Capital Area Federation of Garden Clubs.

Very best garden deals

Montgomery County offers three of the best deals around the metro area for gardeners. According to Joe Keyser, in the county's Department of Environmental Protection, residents can obtain the largest composting bin commercially made for residential use for a mere $5. The bin would sell for at least $19 retail, he said.

County residents and others can purchase the

bins Monday through Friday from 9 a.m. to 5 p.m. at the Audubon Naturalist Society in Chevy Chase (301) 652-9188, the University of Maryland cooperative extension office in Rockville (301) 590-9650, or at any of the five county government centers. For more information, contact the University of Maryland home and garden information center, (800) 342-2507.

The bin, which will last seven to 10 years, can save a resident hundreds of dollars over that time period, Keyser said. The bins hold 24 cubic yards, roughly equivalent to 30 bags of leaves. In the county, if not recycled at the residence, leaves must be placed in paper bags for collection, at a cost of about 50 cents per bag, he said. But the leaves themselves can save a resident money in fertilizer and mulching costs, he added.

The county also runs a coupon program for anyone who attends one of the free composting workshops given through local retailers and the library system. Coupons are given for $15 off grasscycling products at selected retailers. These items include: mulching lawn mowers, blades, or retrofit kits, and composting bins. Officials say that grasscycling, that is, leaving the mowed cuttings on the lawn, saves money by reducing fertilizer and water usage. Call (301) 217-2870.

Free wood chip mulch can be obtained from Montgomery County at nine locations. The sites are self-serve, so anyone throughout the metro area can help themselves to as much mulch as can be hauled away. The stuff is suitable for dressing woody plants and as a cover for walkways and playgrounds.

The locations are: Wheaton Plaza off University Blvd., Watkins Mill High School in Gaithersburg, old Belt Junior High in Aspen Hill, Wheaton Regional Park off Kemp Mill Road, Peary High School in Wheaton, Montgomery County Stump Area near the Trolley Museum in Layhill, Fairland Park in Burtonsville, the Recycling Center at Route 355 and Shady Grove Road in Derwood, and Brookview Elementary School in Hillandale.

County officials recommend that residents let the mulch age for four to six months. However, they said that it can be used right away as well. Horror stories of homeowners finding termites in the mulch are extremely rare, another official said, since the heat of the composted pile where the mulch is stored kills nearly everything even before it is fully aged. In some cases, the mulch may contain allergens like poison oak, so the county recommends wearing gloves when handling it. Fairfax County, Va. also gives away wood mulch, but it is not as accessible. For $35 in Arlington County, Va., county drivers will deliver a truckload of leaf mulch to a resident's door.

Another way to obtain free mulch is to call a tree care company to see if it is doing any business in your area, and if so, ask them to drop it off at your place. In this case, because there is more chance of disease, the material should be composted for at least four months, or merely left to age for about six months before using.

More strategies for saving

Several other strategies for saving were mentioned by the experts interviewed. Keyser and others noted that buying plants through mail order catalogs generally can lead to significant savings. Fruit trees, for example, can be bought in bulk for about one third of the price at a nursery. Such catalogs often have the widest selection at the lowest price.

The fierce competition between home improvement giants Home Depot and Hechinger has driven costs down for basic gardening supplies and standard plants to the lowest levels in years, according to Don Katzen, executive producer of Montgomery Television's cable show *In The Garden*. But the numerous specialized nurseries and smaller mom-and-pop operations in the area by far have a larger selection, he said. Warehouse stores also have good prices on lawn and garden items, but the selection is limited, and the products usually are packaged in larger quantities, he noted.

Good deals can also be had through plant sales at non-profit organizations like the Botanic Gardens and the National Cathedral. One source said this was a nice way to save money and help the group. To acquire native plants that grow in the wild locally, but that may be endangered due to overdevelopment, seek out sales sponsored by groups such as the Virginia Native Plant Society and different botanic gardens. The proceeds of such sales usually go to the conservation and restoration of native plants.

Renting specialized equipment is often the best

way to go to save a few bucks. If you only have one old tree or bush to take down, then it's cheaper to rent a chain saw and do it yourself than to either hire someone else to do it, or buy a chain saw. One local company rents the tool for $40 to $45 per day or $20 to $25 per four hours, depending on the size of the saw. A 16-inch saw at Home Depot would cost between $130 and $150.

Hiring a neighborhood high school or college student, as opposed to contracting with a lawn service is another way to cut down costs. A unique program run by the city of Rockville, Md., refers kids ages 14 to 18 who have been screened, to county residents who need help with mowing, raking leaves, snow removal, and general yard work. The cost ranges from $5 to $15 per hour, and is negotiated through the city, which also arranges transportation for the kids.

Finally, while it is time-consuming to do-it-yourself compared to hiring someone to take over the chore, we postulate, as *The Gardener's Catalogue* simply stated, that "We must always cultivate our garden." (Chauncey would understand.)

Saving at the watering hole

Ah, Summertime, and the livin' is easy. Fish are jumpin' and the water bills are sky high.

With apologies to the Gershwins for altering a lyric, summer water bills can sometimes be as much of a killer financially as the famous D.C.-area heat is on the comfort-index scale. People around here can waste an awful lot of water. And they waste money too—it literally goes down the drain. Metro area residents water (some say, drown!) their lawns (and their sidewalks, unfortunately); they fill backyard pools; they get sweaty and take more and longer showers to cool off; and they run hoses on themselves when they wash their cars.

So, we wondered, "Where can we get the best tips for summertime water conservation?" And the answer came like a flash of lightning on the dusty prairie: "Texas!" Lack of water and water rights are such big issues in the Lone Star State that politicians have found themselves immersed in the subject.

Therefore, it should be no surprise that the Texas Water Development Board (TWDB) has prepared excellent information on outdoor water conservation in hot weather and we hereby pass it on to you somewhat boiled down (pardon the pun).

According to the water board, studies have shown that "the typical lawn often receives twice as much water as required to maintain healthy grass." It offers these tips for outdoor water use:

√ Water lawns early in the morning (4 a.m. to 6 a.m. is recommended to ease strains on the water system, and this is not inconvenient if you have an automatic sprinkler system). Evaporation losses will be up to 60 percent higher later in the day.

√ Do not water on windy days. Set sprinklers so that the lawn, not sidewalks and driveways, is watered. The asphalt, says TWDB, "will never grow a thing."

√ Different types of grass should be watered at different intervals. TWDB's recommendations for the following grasses (we picked out the ones used frequently in the D.C. area) are: Tall Fescue and Bluegrass—every four days; Zoysia and Bermudagrass—every 7-10 days; and Carpetgrass—every five days.

√ Do not "scalp" lawns when mowing during hot weather. Taller grass holds moisture better (TWDB recommends a 1/2" to 3/4" height cut).

√ To avoid excessive evaporation, use a sprinkler that produces large drops of water, rather than a fine mist.

√ Water slowly for better absorption.

√ Choose plant varieties with low water requirements.

√ Consider decorating areas of the lawn with rocks, gravel, wood chips, or other materials that require no water.

√ Do not "sweep" walks and driveways with a hose. Use a broom.

√ Use a bucket of soapy water and use the hose only for rinsing when washing the car or boat.

√ Use a watering can or hand water with the hose in small areas of the lawn that need more frequent watering, such as those near walks or driveways or in especially hot, sunny spots.

√ Repair leaky faucets. Be sure the hose connection to the faucet has a rubber washer and is screwed on tightly.

√ Run the filtered backwash from pools and hot tubs onto the lawn rather than down the drain.

√ Perform good maintenance on your lawn watering equipment to ensure it's working at optimum efficiency.

The water board also offers tips for indoor energy use, such as the use of low-flow devices on faucets and water reduction devices on toilets.

When it comes to taking those lengthy showers we mentioned earlier, however, perhaps the best tip came from a California billboard of the 1970s: "Sing shorter songs." And then pay lower water bills.

Just for Kids (of All Ages)

Chapter 4

LOW-COST SPORTS AND RECREATIONAL equipment and activities can be found throughout our area. This is when being frugal really is fun. This chapter includes listings of local stores as well as ideas for keeping the kids or yourself busy on lazy days.

Toys, (and sporting goods) aren't us, or are they?

Buying and selling used toys and sports equipment is one way to pick up on great bargains or make some extra cash. It's fun, frugal and environmentally friendly to trade in used athletic clothes, equipment or toys for cash or for items that are new to you, like scuba diving equipment, a little red wagon, that blocks set you've always coveted, or a set of golf clubs.

A local newspaper reported recently that the resale toy and sporting goods industry is growing exponentially. An international franchise for sports equipment, Play It Again Sports, reportedly has more than 500 locations nationwide with $200 million in annual sales. Locally, Play It Again Sports can be found at three locations. They are independently owned and operated, so their policies and hours are listed separately below:

- Play It Again Sports, Quince Orchard Plaza, Gaithersburg, Md. (301) 840-1122; Mon-Fri 10-9; Sat 10-6; Sun 11-5. No appointment necessary to drop off. Items under $100 paid outright; others on consignment. Takes exercise equipment and most other sporting goods.
- Play It Again Sports, Laurel Lakes Shopping Center, U.S. Route 1, Laurel, Md., (301) 317-3943; Mon-Fri 10-8:30, Sat 10-6. Also a 40/60 split. No appointment necessary to consign. Does not accept bowling or archery equipment; large exercise equipment accepted, but call first.

A local franchise, Toy Traders, has two stores that will pay by check for toys in good condition, that would look good on the shelf and are complete. According to one shopkeeper we interviewed, customers start buying in August for Christmas and Chanukah, and continue to do so heavily through September and on toward the end of the year. But by November, there aren't enough consignments to keep up with demand, so that is also a good time to bring in items to sell. The stores' locations are:

- Toy Traders, Gaithersburg Square, 536 N. Frederick Ave., Gaithersburg, Md. (301) 258-1023, Mon-Sat 10-8; Sun 12-5.
- Toy Traders, Layhill Shopping Center, 14390 Layhill Road, Silver Spring, Md. (301) 598-5588, Mon.-Sat. 10-5.

> **More signs of the frugal times...**
>
> **"How to Make Money and Save Money."**
>
> (An ad for Exercise Equipment Exchange, which buys and sells used equipment, and is "a new kind of store which turns under-used eqiupment into $$$." They will "take apart and pick up your NordicTracks, LifeCycles, StairMaster, home gyms and other equipment and send you ca$h. In turn, we sell the equipment to people who are looking for maximum exercise results with a minimum of investment... It's that simple," according to the ad.)

Another store, Exercise Equipment Exchange, specializes in indoor athletic or exercise equipment, such as tread mills, bikes, weight sets, stair steppers, and the like.

The establishment has two locations, with the same hours, Thurs 4-8, Fri-Sat 10-8; Sun 12-6:

• Exercise Equipment Exchange, 283 Muddy Branch Rd., Gaithersburg, Md. (301) 869-4EEE.

• Exercise Equipment Exchange, 6671 Backlick Rd., Springfield, Va. (703) 912-4EEE.

For small children, many local clothing consignment shops in the area also carry gently used toys. Such stores tend to carry both women's and children's clothing, as well as a selection of maternity wear. These include, but are by no means limited to, the following stores, some of which are listed elsewhere in this book:

• Kensington Caboose, Kensington, Md. (301) 929-

0178.
- Kids' Stuff, Washington, D.C. (202) 244-2221.
- Paddington Station, Vienna, Va. (703) 938-0378.
- Small Change, Lake Anne, Reston, Va. (703) 437-7730.
- Twice Upon A Child, Sterling, Va (703) 406-0601.

Bargains for frugal students

A good time to start attending to the myriad of back-to-school details is when the summer is about half over. Preparing in advance can make the transition less wrenching later. The old adage that an ounce of prevention is worth a pound of cure is definitely true here. Time, money, and aggravation all can be saved by thinking ahead.

These tips and sources are for area residents both with and without kids, because some parents are going back to school as well to finish up college degrees, or begin graduate or professional degrees.

Get Physical—A good time- and anxiety-saver is to get your children's back-to-school physical examinations done early. Don't wait until a week before school starts. By doing this early when pediatricians' offices are not swamped, you can schedule appointments at times more convenient for you and you can know that your children are up to date on any shots or vaccinations they might need. Many childrens' sports teams require these examinations also.

Buy Smart—Many schools send parents lists of the school supplies their children will need for their particular grade. If you don't get a letter in August telling you what's needed, call the school and see if someone in the office can tell you. School supplies are cheapest in August; once you know what you need to buy, you can watch the newspapers for ads, and watch the yard sales. Watch for coupons too, from such companies as Crayola. Get good-quality book bags. Label everything with name and phone number, so things can be returned if they are lost. Good places for back-to-school supplies include Wal-Mart, Sam's Club and Price Club.

Clothes Make the Student 101—As children get older and peer pressure intensifies, it is not as easy to just dress your kids from yard sales like you could when they were infants or toddlers. Nevertheless, certain basics still can be obtained this way. Watch for solid color turtlenecks, sweatshirts, sweatpants, jeans, slickers, snow boots, ski pants, etc. These latter two items, in particular, can be expensive, especially when one considers that you might only need them a few times over the course of the cold months. But when you need them, you need them. Although it's psychologically difficult to buy down-filled clothing at a yard sale on a 90-degree day, a few months hence you'll be glad you only spent $5 for your 10-year-old's ski pants instead of $40 to $70.

Clothes Make the Student 102—Even the most hard-core thrifty parent may feel it necessary to get a few new, stylish items for kids' back to school wardrobes. But you can find that many items can be filled in by taking stock of last year's clothes, having the child or children try them on to see if they still fit or need to be mended, and then filling in with yard sale/thrift shop merchandise. Discount stores such as T.J. Maxx and Ross—if you get there earlier in the season, such as August—have good prices on back-to-school clothing and bookbags. Also, stores such as Sunny's Surplus can be good sources for jeans, tee shirts and work shirts.

Feed Yourself—In July and August visit Sam's Club, Price Club, the Giant Food Superdeals section, and stock up on peanut butter, jelly, shrink-wrapped multipacks of canned tuna fish and other lunchbox staple items. These can last several months. Also, when yard-saling, watch for overstock merchandise from Tupperware salespersons (of which there are many in the D.C. area) that you can use for packing lunches.

Recycle Containers—It saves both environmentally and financially to pack sandwiches in those hard plastic square cases, to put applesauce in small containers instead of buying prepackaged throwaways. They are often found at yard sales for less than 50 cents each. Savings from cloth napkins can add up, too. Freezable ice packs also are good items to put in lunches, especially during the first few months of school when the weather is still hot and there is greater chance for food spoilage.

Maintain Mechanicals—Avoid mechanical difficulties. Winterize all cars that will be transporting students to school. Among life's most annoying challenges has to be the spectacle of one's car failing to start on a day when you are signed up to help chaperone a field trip, or when you have a 9 a.m. midterm examination at the local community college. Likewise, check out computers and other home office equipment for possible mechanical difficulties before school starts. For working parents, precious hours of annual leave should be used for vacations, not whiling away the hours in repair shops waiting for a mechanical necessity to be returned to you.

Doing the diaper challenge: a dry cost comparison

Going backwards in time a little bit, the cost of diapers is enough to make a new mother cry, especially when she multiplies the price of a pack by the number her baby goes through daily, weekly, monthly, and yearly! Smaller disposable diapers cost less than diapers for a larger child, but the younger infant goes through more of them than an older baby. And what about cloth diapers, even if more environmentally friendly, are they really cheaper?

Comparing prices of diaper services as well as disposables at a variety of stores shows that price, while an important criterion, must be weighed against product performance, which means a proper fit to prevent leaks. And the only way to find out how a particular type of diaper fits, is to try different brands and types to see which one works best for your child. One local drug store's house brand leaked so many times that it gave other house brands a bad name. But we found that the KMart house brand, Luvs, and others performed equally well.

First, a look at diaper services. Cloth diapers through these services in the metro area seemed to be cheaper than disposables in cost per diaper. Some samples:

• Nu-Dy-Per Baby Service - 80 diapers delivered and picked up weekly for $12.50 per week (16 cents per diaper).

• Dy-Dee - 70 diapers delivered and picked up weekly for $11.15 per week (16 cents per diaper).

• Stork Dy-Dee - 90 diapers delivered and picked up weekly for $12 per week (13 cents per diaper).

The list of disposables below is a rough comparison because not every store carried every national brand. And the house brands were different. In addition, a couple of national brands, notably Luvs and Huggies continually seem to run coupon promotions, which can save the consumer another 75 cents to $1 per package.

- **Magruders Grocery Stores**

Huggies Ultratrim 40s for 12-18 pounds 7.99 (20 cents per diaper); Pampers Ultradry 40s for 12-18 pounds 7.99 (20 cents per diaper); Fittis (house brand) 30s for 12-26 pounds 5.99 (20 cents per diaper).

- **Giant Food**

Pampers Ultradry 40s for 12-18 pounds 8.99 (22 cents per diaper); Super G Ultras (house brand) 40s 12-18 pounds 6.99 (17 cents per diaper).

- **Toys R Us**

Huggies Ultratrim 40s for 12-18 pounds 7.99 (20 cents per diaper); Pampers Ultradry 40s for 12-18 pounds 7.99 (20 cents per diaper); Ultras (house brand) 72s for 12-24 pounds 11.49 (16 cents per diaper); Ultras 108s for 12-24 pounds 16.99 (16 cents per diaper).

- **Wal-mart**

Pampers Ultradry 36s for 12-18 pounds 6.96 (19 cents per diaper); Dri-Bottoms 36s for 12-18 pounds 5.97 (17 cents per diaper).

- **KMart**

Huggies Ultratrim 40s for 12-18 pounds 7.99 (20 cents per diaper); Pampers Ultradry 40s for 12-18 pounds 7.99 (20 cents per diaper).

- **Montgomery Ward**
Evenflo Ultra Deluxe Stages 40s for 12 - 18 pounds 5.99 (on sale) (15 cents per diaper).

And there's the *bottom* line on diapers.

20 themes to keep kids un-bored

When school is out in summer, or spring break, and you haven't sent your offspring to computer camp, space camp, karate camp, or some other type of encampment, take a few moments to consider some of these less expensive activities to avoid being assaulted with the words, "Mom/Dad, I'm so BORED. There's nothing to DO."

All of the following suggestions for interesting and fun things for D.C.-area parents and children to do fall into the frugalist category. The metro area is fortunate to have an abundance of low- or no-cost activities that in many cities are far from free.

Camps often have "themes" that intersect with the interests of the children who go there. You can do a lower-cost version of this by planning "theme" weeks, based on something your child or children are interested in. We have set up "Planes and Trains Week" as an example, and then we follow up with 19 other possibilities. The best themes for your needs will be determined by your children's vocations, so be creative!

1. "Planes and Trains Week"

SUNDAY: Freeway Airport, 3900 Church Road, Bowie, Md., a local airport where a number of small plane enthusiasts keep their aircraft, offers flying lessons (301) 390-6424. Or, also on Sundays, one can travel 15 miles south of Warrenton, Va., on Route 17 to the town of Bealton. There, every Sunday through October, stunt flyers put on quite a show, wingwalking on old biplanes, etc. at the Bealton Flying Circus. Admission is $10 for adults, $3 for children. Gates open at 11 a.m. and the show is at 2:30 p.m. Food and biplane rides are sold separately. 1-540-439-8661.

Another alternative (free admission) is the federal Goddard Space Flight Center, a National Aeronautics and Space Administration installation in Greenbelt, Md., where the U.S.' first rockets were designed in the 1950s. Goddard has a visitor's center with museum and exhibits that is open daily 10 a.m. to 4 p.m. Public tours about 45 minutes in length are offered at 11:30 a.m. and 2:30 p.m. Monday through Saturday. Among the exhibits are model rockets and a space capsule that visitors can enter and sit in. Model rocket launches are scheduled for 1 p.m. the first and third Sundays of each month. There is a museum shop. Goddard is accessible via the Baltimore-Washington Parkway.

MONDAY: Take the metro (orange or blue line; it's tough to find parking spaces in D.C.) to the Smithsonian's Air and Space

Museum (free admission), visit some of the best flight exhibits in the world, and take in a movie at the museum's 486-seat Samuel P. Langley Theater. The theater's 50 x 75 feet wide IMAX screen is, says the museum, "the world's largest film format" and the films are breathtaking to see for all ages. The films all depict the wonders of the world and of flight and are less than an hour each. Cost is $3.25 for adults, $2.00 for children aged 2 to 16 years, students with ID and seniors 55 and over. For information on what's playing, call (202) 357-1686. You might consider bringing a (nonperishable) picnic lunch in a backpack and eating out on the Mall, with its view on either end of the Washington Monument and the U.S. Capitol. Then head home and rent a film based on flight (or save the movie rental for another night). Rentable are: Apollo 13, The Great Waldo Pepper, The Spirit of St. Louis and (for older kids) The Right Stuff, to name a few.

TUESDAY: If your kids have never been to a major airport, and they're not too jaded, take the metro out to National Airport and just hang out and watch the planes take off, international visitors arrive, etc. You then could get back on the blue line and visit a few sights along the line, such as Arlington National Cemetery or the Capitol.

WEDNESDAY: You could visit the College Park, Md. Airport, 6709 Corporal Frank Scott Drive, (301) 864-5844. This airport may be the oldest continuously operating airport in the country—it opened in 1909, just six years after the Wright Brothers made their historic flight at Kitty Hawk, N.C. One can visit the airport's observation deck and watch the planes take off and land any time; it's open 24 hours. Children might find the 1940 biplane kept there to be of interest; there also are Cessna 140s and Comanche fighter planes, among others. A museum with free admission offers memorabilia about the airport. The museum is open Wednesday through Friday from 11 a.m. to 3 p.m. and Saturday and Sunday from 11 a.m. to 5 p.m.

THURSDAY: How about a kite-flying day? (Or a frisbee-flying day?) Go to a wide open field (assuming there's at least some breeze) or a less-than-jampacked beach and just have fun!

FRIDAY: Try a trip up Maryland Route 29 (towards Baltimore) and stop off at the Railroad Station Museum in Ellicott City, just north of Columbia. Exhibits include a diorama depicting the trip of Tom Thumb, America's first scheduled passenger train. Adults $3; seniors $2; ages 5 to 12, $1; under 5 are free. Open Friday through Monday 11 a.m. to 4 p.m. Main St. and Maryland Ave. (410) 461-1944. Ellicott City is an old, quaint town that is fun to walk around in also.

SATURDAY: Rock Creek Nature Center offers planetarium shows, Saturday and Sunday at 1 p.m. for ages 4 and up, and at 4 p.m. for ages 7 and up. Free tickets are distributed 30 minutes before showtime. 5200 Glover Rd. N.W.; (202) 426-6829. Also on Saturday and Sunday, the Trolley Museum at Northwest Branch Regional Park (formerly Wheaton Regional Park) offers rides on European and American trolleys. There are exhibits too, which are free. The rides are $2 for adults, $1.50 for kids 2-18, and under 2 are free. Bonifant Road between Layhill Road and New Hampshire Ave., north of Wheaton. (301) 384-6088. Perhaps you can catch a free concert by the Air Force Band or one of its units, such as the Airmen of Note. They usually play at least one or two Air Force songs, in addition to standard summer concert fare.

19 more possible themes

Here are 19 other possible themes for you to flesh out as you see fit. Enjoy!

2. "Learning to Cook" week, culminating in a feast prepared by the children.

3. "Learning to Bake" week. How sweet it is!

4. Music week—abundance of free summer concerts (check papers for listings). Try getting your child to learn the musical instrument of his or her choice with a borrowed instrument. Also, have the child create tapes that are compendiums of the type of music he/she likes; then there will be a cassette tailor-made for his/her interests.

5. Library week—local libraries throughout the area have great summer programs—

storytellers, musicians (helpful to No. 4 above), plays, etc. With a little planning and research (schedules are obtainable easily from the various local library systems), you can see new and interesting performances daily as you roam the local library circuit.

6. "Crafts" week—this might be good prior to the Fourth of July. The kids can make t-shirts or souvenirs for friends and family for the Fourth.

7. Animals week—the National Zoo, the Reston Zoo, the Beltsville Agricultural and Research Center, local horse farms, etc. If you don't mind spending a little more, the Baltimore Aquarium is a great day trip.

8. Art week—visit the National Gallery, the Corcoran, etc. Buy some art supplies and work on a project.

9. Revolutionary War Period Week—Mt. Vernon, James Madison's house, James Monroe's house, Smithsonian Museum of American History.

10. Civil War Week—same modus operandi as No. 9. Manassas and Antietam battlefields. Many historical markers.

11. Garden Week—have the kids pick out seeds to plant; then they can watch vegetables and herbs grow all summer long and enjoy harvesting them in the fall. See the botanical gardens on the Mall and at Northwest Regional Park.

12. Architecture week—craft your own

architectural tour of Washington, go afield to the Eastern Shore and north to Baltimore for different styles. See if the kids would like to keep a journal of what they find interesting, or sketch their own ideas.

13. Archaeology Week—the Smithsonian again, of course; recent archaeological digs in St. Mary's County, in Southern Maryland. National Geographic Building at 17th and M Streets N.W. downtown.

14. Entrepreneur week—have the kids plan and host a yard sale. Do a "matching grant"—for every dollar of merchandise of theirs they sell, pay them a dime in addition to the price they received for the merchandise. Have them do all the organizing, preparing of advertising and merchandise. If they ready your merchandise as well, give them a percentage of the selling price.

15. Baseball week—Babe Ruth's house in Baltimore; minor league baseball with the Frederick Keys and Bowie Baysox (cheaper than the Orioles, but maybe finish up the week at Camden Yards). For kids who play baseball or softball, work at perfecting skills, at a mini "baseball camp day" organized with a few other parents.

16. Water fun week—canoeing, swimming, boating, fishing. Try out different bodies of water.

17. Nature week—birdwatching, "hunting with a camera" for deer, etc.

18. A week of charitable works—help at nursing homes by reading to patients; prepare meals for a soup kitchen; donate leftover garage sale items to a church or homeless shelter.

19. A week of mini-trips—Seven States in Seven Days, and sleep at home at night. Choose points of interest in: Maryland, Virginia, West Virginia, Delaware, Pennsylvania, New Jersey, and D.C.

20. A week of sittin' around doin' nothin.' You're entitled to that too, but let them know that if the word "bored" starts becoming a mantra again, you might have to undertake "Get the House Cleaner and Neater Than It's Ever Been" Week.

Numbers for local library systems

To find out about upcoming events for your library week, or for any other time of the year, the following listing provides the key phone numbers for library systems around our area.

- District of Columbia Public Library System; hours and general information (202) 727-1111; information & reference (202) 727-1126.
- Montgomery County Library System general information (301) 217-4636.
- Prince George's County Library System. Main number (301) 699-3500.

- City of Alexandria, Va., Libraries, main number (703) 838-4558.
- Fairfax City Regional Library, (703) 246-2281.
- City of Falls Church, Mary Riley Styles Public Library (703) 241-5030.
- Arlington County Libraries, (703) 358-5990.
- Fairfax County Libraries, (703) 222-3155.
- Loudoun County Libraries, (703) 777-0368.
- Prince William County Libraries, (703) 792-6100.

Entertainment, Special Days

Chapter 5

THIS CHAPTER FOCUSES ON LOW-COST ENTERTAINMENT; making the most of special occasions like Valentine's Day or President's Day weekend; and a year-round strategy for gift giving that seeks to reduce the sense of panic and the actual overspending that can occur at year-end holiday time.

Washington is not traditionally known as a great place for theater, dance, and music—it is most often thought of as the seat of government, not the heart of culture.

Yet, for those who think their cultural horizons often seem limited to the Kennedy Center, Arena Stage, and the National Theater (because these theaters' productions are advertised the most) we ask (to paraphrase Shakespeare—sort of):

"To pay or not to pay, that is the question ... Is it not nobler in the mind (and easier on the purse) to see an outstanding local theater production than to be strongarmed for $50-per-person tickets and feel awash in a sea of troubles if the high-priced production isn't truly outstanding?"

You see what we mean. For $50 or more per ticket, "fairly enjoyable" just doesn't cut it, the play has got to be great, one thinks. But for $8 to $10 a ticket, one can relax and enjoy a well-produced play or well-played concert even if the production values are less than monumental and the stars aren't Tommy Tune and Julie Andrews.

The D.C. area has numerous semi-professional theater troupes, talented amateur theater groups, community orchestras, opera companies, dance troupes and a variety of other types of inexpensive entertainment.

Another talented segment to consider are the productions of the theater departments and musical ensembles at local universities. Catholic University has a nationally known theater department, for example. Free concerts by military bands are another often-overlooked source of quality entertainment. All the branches of the military have a number of breakdown units of the larger band. These include jazz bands such as the Airmen of Note (Air Force) and the Navy Commodores.

Usher in the savings

Local playwright Eliot Byerrum told us that one sure way to cut down on the cost of theatergoing is to offer to usher.

"If you usher, you get to see the shows for free," the playwright said. According to Byerrum, smaller local theaters such as the Source Theater and Woolly Mammoth Theater do this, and "it never hurts just to call up and ask" any theater that has a play going that you might be interested in seeing.

In addition, Byerrum said, one can call the local professional theaters and ask if they are previewing a play. Preview audience members, she said, often can see a play for nothing or close to nothing. Filling the audience for a play preview is known as "papering" in showbiz, according to this theater insider. Local theater groups abound throughout the area. Some have been around quite awhile. Dinner theaters also can be fairly good bargains when you're looking to take in a full-course meal and a show together. Comedy clubs can be good bargains too. Check your local newspapers for reviews of local theater and music productions.

Another way to cut down the price of some entertainments is through use of so-called Entertainment Books. These sell for $35 or $40, and are usually done as fundraisers through churches, sports clubs, etc. The books contain half-price coupons for dinner theaters, as well as restaurants, and a few other businesses as well.

When you do want to take in a national show or concert in the D.C. area, a frugal option is Ticketplace, at George Washington University Lisner Auditorium, (202) 842-5387, 730 21st St., N.W. (at 21st and H Sts.). Sponsored by the Cultural Alliance of Washington, Ticketplace offers half-priced tickets to concerts and shows on the day of the performance. Hours are 12 to 6 p.m., Tues.-Fri.; 11 a.m. to 5 p.m. Saturday; and closed Sunday and Monday. Tickets for Sunday and Monday shows can be obtained on Saturday. Sales are cash only and a service charge of 10 percent of the full-face value of the ticket is added on.

One semi-philosophical note: Support for the arts begins at the grass roots level; supporting local artists by attending their performances benefits both the arts and one's cultural budget. All the great Broadway stars got their start at the local level (they don't spring full-grown from the brow of Andrew Lloyd Webber) and that's where the stars of tomorrow will come from too.

The principle is the same as in buying clothes. If you only will wear new designer clothes, you might just buy one outfit a year. If you don't mind consignment shops, you can get a range of outfits for the same price.

But after you've spent $100 for two tickets to a show (plus parking and a baby sitter), you might wait before indulging again. If the tickets are $10 each, you might go again next month.

A bounty of local choices

Community orchestras in the area range from the professional to local youth orchestras. Many offer season subscriptions at considerably less money than a subscription for the National Symphony. Some excellent orchestras such as the National Gallery Orchestra perform for free.

Most of the orchestras have season subscriptions for about $45 per person, while National Symphony tickets usually go for $20 to $40 per concert. To name a few examples from different parts of the area:

Washington Symphony Orchestra, $125 for orchestra or $50 for balcony for five-concert 1996-97 season subscription, (202) 857-0970.

Prince George's Philharmonic; five-concert 1996-97 series subscription is $50 for regular unreserved seating, and $32 for seniors and students;

(301) 454-1462. Children ages 6-17 are free.

Alexandria Symphony Orchestra; five-concert 1996-97 season will cost about $85-$105 for regular seating; $50-$75 for students; and $75-$95 for seniors; (703) 845-8005.

Local colleges and universities that have orchestras or chamber groups with student players are listed below with phone numbers to call for schedules and prices. Watch the local papers for fine-print listings of these colleges' and universities' concerts and those of high schools:

- American University, D.C. (202) 885-3420.
- Catholic University, Hartke Theater, D.C. (202) 319-4000.
- George Mason University, Patriot Center, Fairfax, Va. (703) 993-3000.
- George Washington University, Lisner Auditorium, D.C. (202) 994-1500.
- Georgetown University, D.C. (202) 687-3838.
- Howard University, D.C. (202) 806-7198.
- University of Maryland, College Park, Md. Rossbrysh Festival (301) 403-6538 and Tawes Theater 405-2201.
- Montgomery College, Fine Arts Center, Rockville, Md. (301) 279-5301.
- Prince George's Community College, Largo, Md. (301) 322-0444.

The military bands often perform at the Smithsonian or at university auditoriums, particularly in the summertime. Like the wonderful, free-admission Smithsonian museums that Washingtonians often take for granted, these bands are similarly unappreciated. One has to be a very good musician to get hired for these bands and their concerts are enjoyable (don't go there looking for premieres of avant garde works, however; they tend to the traditional).

Movies also can be expensive, but there are bargains to be had there too (aside from a Blockbuster and Orville Redenbacher night, which also can be fine). If you like a real movie theater, try the $2 or 99 cents theaters. They run films that are about to come out on video (or may already be out) but for those who would rather see, say, *Apollo 13* or *Braveheart* on a screen larger than a card table top, the price can't be beat (the concession stands are where they make their money). Suburban cities' civic centers, town halls, libraries, and local high schools are great sources of low-cost movies, lectures, and special interest programs. Some of the more active ones in our area include those listed below.

- Fairfax, Va. Orchestra, annual city celebration day in the old town section, and other events.
- Montgomery County Fair Grounds, Gaithersburg, Md. In addition to the annual agricultural fair in August, the fairgrounds host antiques and craft fairs several times throughout the year, and occasional flea markets.
- Montpelier Mansion, Laurel, Md.
- Reston, Va. Town Center. Offers outdoor concerts, ice-skating in the winter, and craft fairs. Events hotline: (800) 368-TOWN.

- Rockville Civic Center Mansion and Fitzgerald Theater, (301) 309-3340. Programs throughout the year range from free art shows featuring local artists to concerts by the Rockville Community Chorus.
- Strathmore Hall Arts Center, Rockville, Md. (301) 530-0540.

A final note, counties in the suburbs sometimes offer resources for the frugal entertainment seeker, so it's worth keeping an eye out for such locally sponsored events.

Strictly Outdoors

If you are looking for outdoor activities that don't cost a lot, the following listing of parks in the national capital area and numbers to call for more information will serve you well. The list includes state and local parks and recreation centers as well as nature centers. Events and programs are usually free, although sometimes there is a nominal charge, and donations are always welcome.

Maryland Parks

- Maryland State Forests and Parks, camping and program information (410) 461-0052.
- Merkle Wildlife Center near Calvert Cliffs State Park (good place to hunt for fossilized shark teeth) Calvert County, Md. (301) 888-1410.
- Sandy Point State Park (on Chesapeake Bay) (410) 974-2149.
- Montgomery County Department of Parks—park information and permits (301) 495-2525.

- Prince George's County, (301)699-2582 for parking, or 918-8111 for facilities information.

Suburban Maryland Nature Centers
- Brookside (Brookside Gardens), 1400 Glenalin Ave., Wheaton (301) 946-9071.
- Locust Grove, 7777 Democracy Blvd., Bethesda, Md. (301) 299-1990.
- Maydale 1638 Maydale Drive, Silver Spring, Md. (301) 384-9447.
- Meadowside, 5100 Meadowside Lane, Rockville, Md. (301) 924-4141.
- Clearwater Nature Center, 11000 Thrift Rd. (nice name!) Clinton, Md. (301) 297-4575.
- 30th Street Nature Center, Mt. Rainier, Md. (301) 927-2163.
- Watkins Nature Center, 301 Watkins Park Drive, Upper Marlboro, Md. (301) 249-6202.

Maryland Cultural, Historic Facilities
- Agricultural History Farm Park, 18400 Muncaster Rd., Derwood, Md. (301) 948-5053.
- Wheaton Regional Park 2000 Shorefield Rd., Wheaton (historic trolley museum), (301) 946-6396.
- College Park Airport (oldest continuously operating airport in the United States), 6709 Cpl. Frank Scott Drive, College Park, Md. (301) 864-5844.
- Montpelier Cultural Arts Center, 12828 Laurel Bowie Rd., Laurel (301) 953-1993.

Virginia Parks and Nature Centers

- Arlington County park general information (703) 358-4747.
- City of Fairfax parks and recreation, general information (703) 385-7858.
- Fairfax County park general information (703) 246-5700.
- George Washington Grist Mill State Park, 5514 Mt. Vernon Memorial Highway, Alexandria, Va. (703) 780-3383.
- Gulf Branch Nature Center, 3608 N. Military Rd., Arlington, Va. (703) 358-3403.
- Horticulture Center, Green Spring Gardens Park, 4601 Green Spring Rd., Alexandria, Va. (703) 642-5173.
- Hidden Oaks Nature Center, (703) 941-1065.
- Hidden Pond Nature Center (703) 451-9588.
- Huntley Meadows Nature Center (703) 768-2525.
- Long Branch Nature Center, 625 S. Carlin Spring Rd., Arlington, Va. (703) 358-6535.
- Loudoun County parks and recreation general information (703) 478-8407.
- Mason Neck State Park, Lorton, 7301 High Point Rd. (703) 780-3383.
- Riverbend Nature Center, (703) 759-3211.

Federal Parks, Historical Sites

- National Park Service—National Capital

Region (U.S. Department of the Interior) Dial-a-Park (202) 619-7275; General information for D.C. metropolitan area (202) 619-7222.

- Mount Vernon (703) 780-2000.
- National Arboretum (outstanding bonsai tree collection and lovely azaleas in springtime), U.S. Department of Agriculture facility, 3501 New York Ave. N.E., (202) 245-2726.
- Greenbelt Park, Greenbelt, Md. (301) 344-3948.
- Great Falls Park, Va. (703) 285-2964, Great Falls Park, Md. (301) 299-2026.

Special days

Certain days throughout the year call out for a special approach. February is a short month in some ways. It's short on days, it's short on warm weather, and it's got this shortsighted little critter who sticks his head out of his burrow to tell us when spring will arrive.

Despite these shortcomings, tradition tells us that the best thing to give or get on Valentine's Day, February 14, is a dozen long-stemmed roses. The ideas presented here go straight to the heart of many special days. (Some other non-February days may call for such lovely but potentially expensive gifts as well: an anniversary, a birthday, or a graduation.)

This poses a thorny problem for frugal people who hate to waste anything. As lovely as those roses are, it still pains some thrifty souls who tell their beloved as the bouquet is proffered, "Oh, you shouldn't have"—and MEAN it. Not to mention a frugal purchaser's thoughts: "Oh well, I know he/she will just love these roses."

Yet, on Valentine's Day, a dozen long-stemmed roses arranged in a vase can run you about $85. A Rose Express employee told us that in the period NOT between Feb. 1 and Feb. 18, they charge $29.99 for a dozen boxed roses and $49.99 for a vase arrangement. Beginning Feb. 1, however, the prices for both boxed and arranged roses increase steadily until they peak on The Day at $54.99 for boxed roses and $84.99 for an arrangement (plus a $3 to $5 delivery charge in the District; higher elsewhere). And Rose Express deals only in roses and they buy in volume!

Aside from giving candy on special days and promising to send roses later when the "off season" starts, what else can one do that is not exhorbitant but still as lovely? How about trying one of the following ideas?

Bake an easy heart-shaped cake in your beloved's favorite flavors, using the pans you already have—don't buy an expensive, gourmet store heart-shaped pan. Here's how: using one round and one square pan of equivalent sizes, bake a layer cake in each one. When done, cool slightly, and then freeze until the cake is suitable for cutting without falling apart. Cut the round cake in half so that there are two half circles. Place the square cake on a plate in a diamond position and add each half circle to the top left and right of the diamond. Voila, a heart! Cover the joints of the cakes with icing and decorate.

Say it in the papers. All the major and local papers seem to have inexpensive deals for sending your Valentine a classified message, such as "Roses aren't cheap, and you know I'm thrifty, I love you forever, and think that you're nifty!" Papers also run these special ad promotions on Mother's Day, Father's Day, and graduation time in mid-June. For the price of the roses, you could publish an epic poem dedicated to your true love in the classifieds!

Craft your own ideas for a gift. If you're creative with crafts, pick up inexpensive, quality materials at local specialty stores such as Ben Franklin, MJDesigns, or Frank's Nursery and Crafts, among others. Jo-Ann's Fabric Stores and Frank's Nursery and Crafts stores are all over the metro area. Another resource is Visual Systems, which caters to graphic artists and recently opened a discount outlet in Laurel, Md. Have a field day with crochet heart boxes ranging from 79 cents to $2.49 and twig heart baskets from 47 cents to $1.47 at Ben's; silk flowers starting at 99 cents at MJD; and gold painted cherubs for under $4.

Free excursions. Wanna see a cherub up close? Try a late afternoon trip to the National Gallery of Art West, 6th and Constitution, which closes at 5 p.m. Monday-Saturday, and 6 p.m. on Sunday, and see how some of the world's greatest artists have depicted lovers through the ages.

Obtain an antique store find that makes a unique gift. Find a place in your heart for these

> **More signs of the frugal times**
>
> **"Are you paying for tomorrow when the day after is so much cheaper?"**
>
> (Wild and frugal logic from, who else, the U.S. Postal Service, in an advertisement for two-day delivery priority mail service. At $3 for up to two pounds in the Mid-Atlantic region, maybe it pays to wait a day after all, rather than sending out a package overnight.)

classics (We found all of these on a trip to Frederick, Md.): Old sheet music, with titles such as "It's Love, Love, Love," "Now You're In My Arms," and "Love Serenade"; a porcelain heart-shaped box for $4; antique Valentine cards for $1; or a red glass candy jar for $11.

Mail a specially stamped Valentine. Several post offices around the country offer a special Valentine's postmark. For delivery on the big day, address the card as you normally would, and include regular postage. Then put it into a larger envelope with a note requesting the special postmark, and mail it by February 9 to the following post office: Postmaster, Loveville, MD 20656 (in St. Mary's County).

The Velvet Rosebush. Ben Franklin Craft stores have for sale during the Heart Holiday season a gorgeous bouquet called "the velvet rosebush." These have been on sale for $3.99 during the last week in January, but even at full-price retail, the bouquet is $9.99, according to an employee. It looks real, consisting of nine red velvet roses bound from the bottom, together with greenery. You could buy a Durand lead crystal vase for $50 or a Wedgwood china vase for $75 at a prominent local department store to put these roses in and you'll still come out ahead rose-wise (if not frugal-wise). Or you could buy a simple glass vase, and use the leftover money for a dress size's worth of Godiva chocolates (although we prefer Fannie Mae—they taste great at less than half the price of gourmet candies).

Gift Baskets. Giant Food stores has ready-made gift baskets, ranging in price. These include baskets with Valentine teddy bears (you know, holding a furry red heart, awwww) and bottles of a sparkling beverage for about $17; "Pamper Your Baby" packages with bubble bath for about $27; and others.

Street Vendor Roses. Roses deemed unacceptable for flower shops often are sold on street corners and at metro stops for about five dollars a half dozen, during most of the year.. This price is usually upped to $10 a half-dozen on Valentine's Day, but this might not be a bad idea. These roses don't last as long as flower shop roses, but they'll still look good on the big day. At grocery store flower shops, one can put together a bouquet with four or five roses, filling in with the less expensive flowers, and then choosing the amount of baby's breath or other trimmings to complete it, for considerably less than the florist variety. (Frugal hint: Hairspray on the blossoms makes cut flowers last longer.)

Presidents' Day sales avoidance

While we lay no claims to being Presidential scholars, we suspect that both George Washington—who toughed it out at Valley Forge and declined the opportunity to be crowned king; and Abe Lincoln—who walked miles to school, studied by candlelight and split rails to make money to further his education—would have understood and approved of the benefits of the frugal lifestyle.

Frugality appears to have been the norm, not the exception, during the two previous centuries. Our research also yielded pertinent quotes on the topic from Washington's fellow Founding Father Thomas Jefferson—our third president; and from Ulysses S. Grant, Lincoln's commanding general in the Civil War and our 18th President. Jefferson called for "a wise and frugal government" in his first inaugural address in 1801. Grant noted in a speech given during his own presidency that the Pilgrims "cultivated industry and frugality at the same time—which is the real foundation of the greatness of the Pilgrims."

Keeping these historical notes in mind, we respectfully suggest that spending wads of cash and plastic the long holiday weekend in February (or any other weekend, for that matter) as retailers would like us to do during the Presidents' Days sales is not nearly as memorable a way to celebrate Washington's and Lincoln's birthdays, as is partaking of the fine commemorations planned in the two presidents' honor in Washington, D.C., the city where they served the nation. While good bargains can no doubt be found at such sales, it may be best to avoid them or spend fewer hours devoted to them.

What follows are the major sights of annual activities during Presidents Day.

- Mt. Vernon—George Washington's home is open every day of the year/Nov. to Feb. 9 a.m. to 4 p.m./April through Aug. 8 a.m. to 5 p.m./ Sept. and Oct. 9 a.m. to 5 p.m. Ordinarily admission charge is $7 for adults, $6 for seniors age 62 and over with ID, and $3 for children ages 6 to 11. On the President's Monday, however, Mt. Vernon is open free to the general public (9 a.m. to 4 p.m.), and special activities are planned. In past years these have included "free samples" breakfast of foods such as those Washington might have eaten, such as hoecakes; laying of a wreath on Washington's tomb by the Commanding General of the Military District; and the Old Guard Fife and Drum Corps performing on Bowling Green. Arrive early to find parking on the grounds, where there are two large parking lots; there also is a shuttlebus from nearby Good Shepherd Church. Phone number for Mt. Vernon is (703) 780-2000.

- Lincoln Memorial—On the actual anniversary of Lincoln's birth, Feb. 12, there typically occurs an annual wreath-laying ceremony at the Lincoln Memorial. The President and Vice President are always invited to attend, and often it is the Vice President who comes, although this is not known for sure until the last minute, according to a spokeswoman. A number of members of Congress, members of the diplomatic corps, and other dignitaries attend, and one of them reads the

Gettysburg Address.

• Washington Monument—On Feb. 22, the actual date of Washington's birth, at 11 a.m. there typically is a wreath-laying ceremony at the Washington Monument. The Old Guard Fife and Drum Corps also may appear here (and at the Lincoln Memorial ceremony as well; they get around).

White House greetings

A prominent greeting card company likes to close its television commercials with the slogan, "When you care enough to send the very best." We believe that the "very best" doesn't have to cost the very most.

We prefer to buy cards at resale shops (unused, of course!), rather than shell out anywhere from $1.50 to $5 per card. So, when we found out the White House had an office specifically for sending out greeting cards for special occasions, we investigated.

According to a staffer in the White House Greetings Office, they will send birthday greetings to anyone 80 years or older; wedding anniversary greetings for couples married 50 years or more; congratulations on the birth of a child; get well cards; condolences; some graduations; and congrats on making Eagle Scout. If you ask, they will also throw in a photo of the president.

Simply send your request in writing by fax to (202) 395-1232; or by mail to: Greetings Office, Room 39, The White House, Washington, D.C. 20500.

Be sure to include with your request the names and addresses of the pertinent people and key dates. For example, an anniversary greeting should specify the couple's names, address to send it to, and date needed. In the case of a new baby, specify the parent's and the child's names and the date the child was born.

While this service is "free," it is an example of your taxpayer dollars at work. And in the present budget- tightening climate, who knows how much longer this special tradition will continue?

If you really want to gauge what inflation has done to our spending power over the years, check the price of greeting cards. It is possible that the reason stores such as Wal-Mart, Giant, and now CVS are advertising up to 40 percent discounts on greeting cards is that customers may be getting a tad annoyed at shelling out $2 for a simple card. Those of us who came of age in earlier eras probably secretly feel that greeting cards should cost about a quarter.

Thrift and consignment shops throughout the metro area frequently offer unused greeting cards for anywhere from 10 cents to 50 cents each. Sometimes, these are extras or overstocks from card shops. Often they are cards someone bought but never sent. Yard sales also are good sources for cards, invitations, and stationery. Some of these are of an earlier era, which can make them seem cute and/or nostalgic. By having a stash of these on hand, you can send out a unique card at a fraction of the cost, and save time by eliminating last-minute trips to the nearest drug store or card shop.

Alternatively, there are several Factory Card Outlet stores in the area where every card is 39 cents. The locations include: Wheaton, Md., Chantilly, Va., Penn Station, Md., Laurel, Md., Mt. Vernon, Va., Gaithersburg, Md., and Alexandria, Va.

A year round gift giving strategy

Gift giving takes place year round, not just at the end of the year. But for many people, year-end celebrations such as Christmas and Chanukah, make the bills for presents bestowed during this season an annual punch in the old pocketbook. And retail industry analysts estimate that many store owners earn 50 percent of their annual profits during the holiday season alone.

Judging from the year-end editions of catalogues stuffing the mailbox and the displays in the stores, when many of us have just gotten our pictures developed from our summer vacations, the holidays already seem to be upon us.

The holiday commercial season seems to start earlier each year and as the actual days or days of celebration draws near, people often tend to: a) panic because they haven't gotten gifts for everyone yet and then b) overspend at the stores in the weeks prior because they haven't gotten gifts for everyone yet, and then c) do last-minute shopping. This often leaves them feeling: 1) guilty that they didn't plan better and shop earlier; 2) guilty that they spent too much money; and 3) angry because the gifts still don't seem "perfect" enough.

But a very large percentage of retailers' business each year is done during the holiday season. This scenario suits retail merchants just fine—we panic and they profit.

It doesn't have to be this way. The gifts that are appreciated the most are not the ones that scream "I'm expensive!" but the ones that evoke the following (silent, often, but heartfelt) response: "Someone really was thinking of my likes and needs when they chose this gift." That's why most people would rather have a small appropriate gift than cash; one says you took the time to think about the person, the other does not indicate that. Personalization is the key (and we don't mean monogramming either).

Acknowledging that the holidays can be a budget buster is the first step toward reining in costs. The second step is making a list of known and potential gift recipients, including people for whom birthdays, weddings, anniversaries, new babies, retirements and other occasions are expected during the year. The third is setting a budget, including some leeway for the inevitable surprise gift giving occasion.

Year-round planning and action can lead to truly special gifts for all the people on your list at a price you can afford. Among the best places to shop are the annual, once-a-year local events. For example, there are the very popular metro-area book sales at:

- Vassar College book sale during the spring, usually held in a government building in downtown D.C.; and
- State Department book sale in the sum-

mer

Other gift gathering options in the Washington area are craft fairs that flourish in September and October. Of course, November and December bring the innumerable church bazaars with their bake sales and white elephant rummage sales.

Catalogs delivered to your home throughout the year can provide an easy and convenient way to shop without time constraints. Catalogs have the added advantage of offering a multitude of ideas for gifts you can copy at a cheaper price by making yourself.

At the very least, catalogs provide a good reference for prices of items you are considering giving that you can compare with local stores and other catalogs. At their best, they can provide convenient, inexpensive, useful or whimsical, perfect gifts that can be delivered directly to the recipient's door.

A catalog of catalogs can be obtained by contacting the Direct Marketing Association, and asking them for the *Great Catalog Guide*, which contains listings of 200 catalogs and 50 product categories. The cost is $3. The address is: 1101 17th St., NW, Suite 705, Washington, D.C. 20036-4704.

Singing the frugal song

Compact discs and audio tapes containing music, books-on-tape, and educational or inspirational recordings are popular gifts.

Yet the gift of music need not break your heart like an old melody. The following list includes stores that sell used compact discs, records, tapes, and miscellaneous items, such as tape cases and cassette organizers. Many of these stores also buy much of their inventory from regular folks. So when you're tired of hearing that same old song, trade it in for a new one and earn a few bucks.

- Bonifant Books (see book store listing in Chapter 6).
- CD Mania, 1083 Wisconsin Ave N.W. (202) 337-4979.
- High Tech Service & Exchange, 228 W. Broad St., Falls Church, Va. (703) 534-1754; Mon-Fri 11-8; Sat 10-6, Sun 12-5.
- House of Musical Traditions, 7040 Carroll Ave., Takoma Park, Md. (301) 270-9090. Tue-Wed 12-7; Thur-Fri Noon-8; Sat 11-7; Sun 11-5; closed Mon.
- Memory Lane Music, 2817 Walters Lane, Forestville, Md. (301) 568-5044; Mon-Sat 11-6, closed Sun.
- Phantasmagoria, 11308 Grandview Ave, Wheaton, Md. (301) 949-8886, 10-9 p.m. Mon-Sat, Sun 11-6.
- Phantasmagoria, 1619 Conn. Ave. NW, at Dupont Circle (202) 462-8886. 10-10 Sun-Tues; 10-11 Wed-Sat.
- P&L Compact Discs, 153 Glyndon St., Vienna, Va. (703) 281-7575; Mon, Wed & Fri 11-8; Tues & Thurs & Sat 11-7; Sun 12-5.
- Record & Tape Exchange, 9448 Main St., Fairfax, Va. (703) 425-4256; Mon-Sat 10-9; Sun 12-6.

- Roadhouse Oldies, 958 Thayer Ave., Silver Spring, Md. (301) 587-1858; Sun 12-4; Mon 12-6; Tues-Fri 12-8; Sat 11-7.
- Second Story Books & Antiques (see bookstore listing in Chapter 6).
- The Record Mart, 217 King St., Alexandria, Va. (703) 683-4583; Mon-Thurs 10-9; Fri & Sat 10-10. Sun 10-7.
- Yesterday & Today Records, 1327-J Rockville Pike, Rockville, Md. (301 279-7007; 11-6 Mon-Sat; 12-6 Sun.

Looking a gift list in the mouth

Most people laugh when someone says (usually at Thanksgiving) that they have completed their holiday shopping. While that situation is ideal, it is difficult for busy Washingtonians. But these suggestions, even if only a few are utilized, can lower one's holiday expenditures while increasing the true value of a present precisely because you have taken the time and trouble to do so.

For example, gifts for a baby's first Christmas or Chanukah that the baby won't outgrow may include: proof set of coins issued in the year of the birth (this gift is the least expensive when purchased during that first year); commemorative stamps, perhaps framed, issued in the year of baby's birth; a newspaper from baby's birthplace on the date of baby's birth; and an enlarged framed picture of the baby.

Gifts for children any time of the year that don't cost a lot are the following: a trunk containing dress-up items such as costume jewelry and grown-up clothes obtained from yard sales; a trip to a place the child would like to visit, such as the zoo or aquarium; a magazine subscription in the child's field of interest, even to magazines usually read by adults, such as *Archaeology Magazine* (kids love to get mail and it makes them feel important); an address book with child's name written on it by you with fabric paint or glitter; and beginning or adding to a collection.

Of course, by spending wisely throughout the year, the gift giver gives his or her budget a boost by amortizing the costs incurred. Some people enjoy the hustle and bustle of gift shopping in December. If you're not one of them, try some of these non-mall suggestions:

√ Gift certificates to movies, restaurants, beauty salons, recreation/athletic centers;

√ Membership to a grocery/warehouse club (about $25 to $35);

√ Magazine/newsletter subscriptions;

√ Something of your own that the recipient has said he/she likes very much;

√ Set of coins;

√ Collectible stamps, or savings bonds;

√ Make a monetary contribution to the recipient's favorite charity, special organization, or worthy cause in his/her name;

√ An old, used book about the recipient's favorite subject;

√ Homemade food goodies;

√ A food basket put together by you from the grocery store;

√ A book of family recipes: ask family members to send you their one best recipe, compile them into a family cookbook, and send out nationwide (an instant priceless herloom!);

√ A membership to a group or institution in the recipient's interest area, such as a particular museum;

√ Homemade goodies to eat packed into tins that might reflect an interest of the recipient (the tins can be obtained through secondhand shopping throughout the year);

√ Coupons to perform a personal service for a friend, e.g. paint an old chair, babysit on a Saturday night, landscaping, car detailing, or whatever would be a special treat (these, by the way, make excellent last minute gifts and are much better than buying hankies at the all-night drug store); and

√ Photographs, especially enlargements that can be made through most grocery stores.

Wrapping it up

In selecting a frugal, fast way to wrap up those gifts, focus on items already available in your home. Amazingly, these types of wrappings often turn out to be more elegant and festive than most of the store-bought kinds. They also can be combined with store wrappings.

Frugal wrappings may include leftover fabric, ribbons, old linens, traditional/formal cloth napkins, and Christmas tree ornaments, garlands, or other seasonal decorations that you no longer want or need. Quite decorative gift coverings can often be made by gathering together several of the same types of items on a package, for instance, old buttons, bows of unused ribbons, and old greeting cards creatively cut up.

For food gifts, try using kitchen twine and cinnamon sticks to tie a loaf of bread to a new cutting board, or a half-dozen muffins to a pretty hotpad. Brown or white paper bags that are plain on one side can be taped up and decorated with living foliage from outside such as holly leaves and berries or pine cones. And maps, newspapers, magazines can be chosen to reflect the tastes or interests of the gift recipient, or the mood of the giver.

Now *that's* a wrap!

Treasure Hunting

Chapter 6

PRAGMATISTS THAT WE ARE, on the lookout for things we can use today, frugalists often overlook the items of collectible or antique value that abound at area thrift stores and yard sales, second hand shops, and antique outlets, and our own closets. That's right, we're talking about "collectibles." These items are the things people used 15 or 20 or 50 years ago, perhaps on a daily basis, but now have been replaced by newer, though not always improved, versions.

Take for instance those corn husk salt and pepper shakers; they may be "instant" collectibles! Most people probably threw theirs out, stuffed them in a storage box, or gave them away. But such objects may be worth a lot to a collector.

That old, hand appliqued quilt from the 1940s may very possibly constitute a great catch for someone. Or how about the illustrated children's book you inherited from a great aunt? Depending on the condition, it could be worth more than you think.

These items can be found at most of the haunts frequented by capital area frugalists. Their value and collectibility, according to local experts, will be determined by the item's condition, and the terms set by the buyer and the seller.

What's a collectible?

A collectible is in the eye of the collector, according to Roger Lund, proprietor of A.B.'s Consignments and Collectibles in Kensington, Md. who spoke at a Bethesda Library program.

"It can be fun and it can be maddening," Lund said. He suggested prospective collectors first decide what to collect, then determine where they will house their collection. For example, he said, if you choose to collect Early American spinning wheels, large wooden contraptions, you will need a very large room to house them in!

Then prospective collectors should ask themselves where can they find the items and whether they can afford to collect, he said. He noted for example that different types of dinnerware can range widely in price, but a collector can soon discover through research and shopping whether a particular type is within his or her price range.

Lund advises people to research the object of their desire to see what's out there and how much some dealers are asking for it. But he cautioned that there is no single definitive book on any particular collectible subject. "Nobody in this business knows everything," he said. Everyone involved in a transaction needs to be happy with the buying and selling price, he remarked.

The condition of any item will influence the price that can be gotten for it, Lund said. Consignors should make an item look as good as possible without harming the integrity of a piece, before taking it to a consignment shop.

Who's a collector?

People who consign collectibles may be dealers, yard salers, or just regular people who have recently cleaned out their closets, according to Lund.

Alice Geiger of the Bethesda Quilters, speaking at the same program, said she was drawn to collecting quilts because they represented women's roles in earlier times. She showed off several stunning handmade quilts from the mid to late 1800s and the 1930s and 1940s.

Some of Geiger's quilts have been dated by Smithsonian Museum experts. She said because of the fragile material, the condition of a quilt is not always an indicator of value. This folk art is often a telling piece of history. Some quilts tell the story of the people who made them and their families. Others describe the times in which they were made, the popular fashions and fabrics of the day, the places people lived, and the simple meaning or importance of every day items.

The May 1995 issue of *Country Living* magazine noted that advertising memorabilia is currently one of the most popular forms of collectible.

"Although nostalgia has motivated countless collectors to buy antiques, few fields are more driven by a yearning to preserve a portion of the past than advertising memorabilia," according to the article, "Advertising Art," by Bruce E. Johnson. The article listed a Betsy Ross tea container valued at $30 and Coca Cola trays valued at $1,250, among other finds.

Book lovers

"If location, location, location is the axiom of real estate, condition, condition, condition is the axiom of book collecting," according to Allan Stypeck, owner of Second Story Books, and book enthusiast extraordinaire.

To collect, Stypeck said at the Bethesda Library program, one must either have a desire to collect for appreciation and enjoyment of books, or for monetary gain. People should only collect books they are interested in, he suggested.

"This is a business basically built out of love. It's subjective," he says. Some elements, are universal, however. In looking for collectible books, Stypeck said the highest prices are usually paid for those with a clean dust jacket and those marked with a first edition identification.

Sometimes a library date stamp on a book will detract from its value. But other times, for instance, if the stamp fairly conclusively indicates a book's age, it can increase the value. He cited an instance in which a date stamp dated a book at 400 years old.

Stypeck noted that an autograph can rarely be authenticated, despite the plethora of books and experts on the subject, but they are still widely sought. For example, President Kennedy was known to have had 1,100 phoney signatures from autopens, secretaries, and the like, he said.

The Washington area is blessed with resources for book collectors such as the Library of Congress, and the National Institutes of Health library, according to Stypeck..

A tip for books with mildew, is not to let them near other books, since the mildew will spread. To eliminate the mildew, Stypeck suggests putting the book under non-chlorophyll kitty litter for two or three days. While the mildew will be destroyed, the stain will remain on the book, he said.

Benjamin Franklin wrote in 1736 that "Wealth is not his who has it, but his who enjoys it." For a collector, enjoying wealth can come from books, old soda bottles, gas station memorabilia, baseball cards, tea tins, and just about anything else—all that stuff that frugalists regularly see in their travels through the yard sale-secondhand store demimonde.

Listing of used book sellers

• Second Story Books — 2000 P St. N.W. Dupont Circle, D.C. (202) 659-8884. 10 a.m. to 10 p.m. 7 days a week.

• Second Story Books (Warehouse) 12160 Parklawn Drive, Rockville, Md. (301) 770-0477. Sun-Thurs 10 a.m. to 7 p.m., Friday and Saturday 10 a.m. to 9 p.m.

• Second Story Books 4836 Bethesda Ave., Bethesda, Md. (301) 656-0170. 10 a.m. to 10 p.m. 7 days a week.

• Book Stop, Bradlee Shopping Center (facing Braddock Rd.), 3640-A King St., Alexandria, Va. (703) 578-3292. 12-6 Mon, Tues, Wed and Fri, 11-6 Sat., 1-5 Sundays. Closed Thursdays.

• Bonifant Books, 11240 Georgia Ave., Wheaton, Md. (301) 946-1526. Mon-Fri 10-8, Sat

10-6, Sundays 11-6.

- Book Alcove, 706 Rockville Pike, Rockville, Md. (301) 309-1231; Monday thru Sat 10-9; 12-6 Sunday.
- Book Ends, Fri thru Mon 12-6, Closed Tue, Wed, Thurs, 2710 Washington Blvd, Arlington, Va. (703) 524-4976.
- Book Rack, 9559 Braddock Rd., Fairfax, Va. (703) 323-0498 M-W 10-8; Thurs-Sat 10-9; Sun 12-5; 7877 Heritage Drive, Annandale, Va. (703) 941-6015; Mon-Thurs 10-7; 10-6 on Fri and Sat; 12-5 Sunday. Interesting frugal note: These stores are part of a chain that was founded by a single mother 33 years ago; they carry mostly paperbacks.
- Felicia's Books, 7627-A Fullerton Rd., Springfield, Va. (703) 866-3966; hours are Mon-Fri 10-6; Sat 10-4.
- Leaf Through, 1701-L Rockville Pike, Rockville, Md. (301) 230-8998; hours are Tues, Weds, Fri 10-7; thurs 10-8, Sat 10-5, Sun 12-5.
- Washington Used Book Center, 11910 Parklawn Drive,

Hot Collectibles

- Advertising Art especially Coca Cola Co., and gasoline stations
- Railroad China
- Dinnerware
- Airline memorabilia especially from defunct carriers, including wings for kids, and flatware
- Unusual sterling silver serving pieces such as an asparagus spoon
- Small animal figurines
- African-American memorabilia
- Postwar Japanese items that say "Made in Japan"
- Perfume bottles
- Head vases from the 1930s
- Costume jewelry
- Sewing notions
- Christmas ornaments
- Old Disney items

Rockville, Md. (301) 984-7358.

- McKay Books, 14245 Lee Highway, Centreville, Va. (703) 830-4048, Mon-Sat 9-9; Sun 11-7; Westgate Shopping Center, 8079 Sudley Rd., Manassas, Va. (in Westgate Shopping Center) (703) 361-9042; same hrs.
- Lantern Bryn Mawr Bookshop, 3222 O St. N.W., Washington, D.C. (202) 333-3222. Mon-Fri 11-4; Sat 11-5; Sun 12-4.

Story of a book

There are two major reasons people frequent yard sales and flea markets (besides just the all-out thrill of it all): yard salers are probably divided about equally between practical folks looking for household items, clothing, etc., and antique dealers and fanciers hunting for treasures.

Then of course there are practical folks keeping an eye out for Meissen china and first editions of *The Great Gatsby*, and antique hunters not averse to picking up a blouse for a dollar if it strikes their fancy.

With the yard sale and flea market season always nearly upon us, we offer some ideas about why it is a good idea to keep your eyes peeled for treasures.

We begin with the story of a book. The book is one you've probably heard of—Ian Fleming's *The Man With the Golden Gun*. An author of this book found a first printing copy for 50 cents at a yard sale (it has an eyecatching dust jacket with fake bullet holes in it, which is why she bought it).

She ended up selling it to a book dealer for $10 after a little (admittedly not extensive) research into what it was worth. (Because it was Ian Fleming's last James Bond book it was not worth as much as some of his other works.) Still, it was a profit of 2000 percent, which beats a lot of investments.

Veteran yard salers and thrift shoppers know that antique dealers and book dealers are often the first ones to show up at 6 a.m. at a yard sale advertised to start at 8 a.m. "You shoulda been here an hour ago," the yard sale proprietor says to the respectful customers who pull up at 7:55 a.m., feeling guilty for being five minutes early. "Some guy came here and bought all these old Disney toys that belonged to my aunt. He gave me $25 for them!" Ouch.

Dealers do this for obvious reasons—they want first crack at any "finds" they can resell at the best profits they can get, but no antique dealer can know everything about all types of antiques and there are always finds to be found, even if you decide you'd rather not be part of the yard sale and flea market "dawn patrol."

Diplomacy and frugality

The British Embassy for the past 15 years has issued a monthly list of items for sale. Most of these are the possessions of diplomats—from a range of embassies—whose tours of duty in the United States are ending.

The list is a compendium of classified ads slotted into three categories—Wheelies, Goods &

Chattels, and Personal Advertisements (tutoring, vacation homes for rent, etc.). It is printed in small type to save paper (frugalists, please note), according to British Embassy staff person Marianne Hosea.

Hosea, who has prepared the list for publication for the last 10 years, said that anyone can pick up the list in person at the embassy's front desk. If you want to have it mailed to you, send a self-addressed stamped envelope to: Ms. Marianne Hosea, Room 204, British Embassy, 3100 Massachusetts Ave., Washington, D.C. 20008.

Chances are that cars and vans being sold through the list are not being unloaded because they are lemons, but because their specifications are not acceptable in an owner's native country (or that shipping an auto is impracticable).

Likewise, furnishings, office equipment, etc., may not be needed back home. Hosea noted that diplomats from all over D.C. advertise in the British Embassy's list, adding that she knows of no other embassy that has such a list. According to Hosea, most embassy tours of duty are either three years for defense personnel, or "two plus two" year tours of duty for other personnel, so most items are relatively new. Some U.S. government agency employees also advertise in the list, she said.

Hosea added that readers of the list "can pick up a bargain when someone has been short-toured" and unexpectedly sent back early.

A perusal of one month's list showed a number of bargains in various categories. Each entry includes the name and office or home telephone numbers of the advertiser. The embassy takes no responsibility for, and does not guarantee, any of the items or services advertised. The items ranged from the prosaic (toasters, irons) to the exotic (handmade rosewood furniture from China, Persian rugs) with many points in between.

Some of the ads also make interesting cross-cultural reading. For example, while a typical American used car ad might say something like, "Have all service receipts," one ad in the embassy's list states, "This vehicle has been serviced at the correct intervals." A 1991 Dodge Spirit is described as being "mostly highway bred" (sure it's not a Ford Mustang?)

But we digress. A sampling of bargain items follows: Xerox memory typewriter, original cost $900, $175 or best offer. "Assorted electrical items ... as a package" for $50 (includes clock radios, iron, coffee machine, timer switches, extension cords, toasters, etc. — sounds like a good gift for that college student in his or her first apartment!); "1987 Mazda 626 LS, book price $4325, sell for $3300."

The length of the list averages a little more than four pages, Hosea said. The list comes out on (approximately) the third of each month.

Guides to antiques

There are a number of antique guides (Kovel's is the most well-known) to help educate oneself about antiques and collectibles. Just frequenting antique shops and taking note of what the dealers are asking is also helpful, especially if you focus on one area or set of areas that you are interested in. Washington-area residents have one additional resource that is invaluable in helping educate themselves about the value of any finds—the Library of Congress.

Nearly every book in the world can be found there, and any member of the public can go to the library and search out the best in reference materials. We were able to research the value of some of yard sale-find books by looking at volumes of *American Book Prices Current* for 1993, 1992, etc. back to 1978. These volumes (Alcove 7, main reading room at the Library) list the prices various rare or collectible books sold for at auction during the year covered. The book was not available at local libraries or bookstores. Borders bookstore downtown said it could be ordered —for $129.95.

A helpful employee in the Library of Congress' rare book room advised book lovers to inventory their books, then check them against the *American Book Prices Current* volumes to know what they may have sold for. Then, he advised, "shop" the books around to several antiquarian book dealers to see who would give the best price.

One dealer told us the Ian Fleming book would sell for about $20, but he had a lot of Ian Fleming right now and wouldn't pay more than a dollar or two for it. But another dealer subsequently bought it for $10.

When one is in garage sale mode, it helps to know a little bit about what might be collectible (nearly everything, it seems), and to trust your intuition. Even if you're just looking for baby clothes or a rototiller, if you see a piece of Nippon china or an old quilt for very little money, you might want to go ahead and get it if you're willing to investigate where you might sell it for a little profit.

Art & Antiques magazine, a beautifully presented and illustrated monthly publication whose articles mainly deal with expensive and rare art and antiques, regularly includes two- and three-paragraph short articles (usually with a picture) on garage sale and flea market finds of as little as $5 that ended up being worth thousands. Ah yes, the treasure hunting instinct runs deep in the human psyche.

The art of garage sales

The April 1995 issue of *Art & Antiques* had an interesting feature written by Stanford A. Tharp, a self-described not-rich man who had an exhibit of the artworks he has collected over the past 30 years.

His finds are solely from garage sales, thrift shops, and flea markets and he is proud of it. He called his show, "Rescue the Perishing: Works of Art Salvaged from Ruin in the Stanford A. Tharp Collection." It was on view at the Frederick R. Weisman Museum at Pepperdine University in Malibu, Calif. in April 1995. What a thrill it must have been for him!

Tharp had a few tidbits of advice for those who share his passion for seeking out finds amid the flotsam at yard sales, flea markets, and what he likes to call "treasure shops." He says to:

√ Shop often, because there is a lot of turnover at thrift shops;

√ Trust your intuition;

√ Don't let the junk around you deter you from plucking your find—visualize it in the exact place you want to put it;

√ Look through boxes because the treasures are often hidden;

√ Don't lay it down if you think you want it because someone else might grab it;

√ Take a magnifying glass (a cheap one will do) to search for dates, signatures, and we add, hallmarks, and

√ Enjoy yourself!

Where fleas dare to tread

Besides Eastern Market's flea market (highlighted in the next chapter, Community Focus) the Washington metro area offers several other larger flea markets. The majority of them are designed for the average person who wants to sell off the usual stuff gathering dust in the garage, attic, or closet. Their prices tend to be competitive. In fact, flea markets can sometimes yield the best bargains because so many people are selling so much stuff at the same time.

But flea markets also tend to attract a fair share of dealers; people who make part or all of their living selling collectibles, antiques, clothes, office supplies, crafts, you-name-it. Their prices tend to be higher, due to overhead costs of running a business. Yet many of them will gladly haggle over the price of their wares at flea markets or swap meets.

Perhaps the best advice for bargain hunters going to a flea market is to get there as soon as it opens and take a quick survey of all the vendors without buying anything. Then, go back to the ones you found interesting and you may be able to do a bit of comparison shopping by already having a feel for whether the person three spaces down has a similar item. This approach also helps you to avoid buyer's fever or getting caught up in the excitement of the event.

The following flea markets operate seasonally in our area, generally from May through October; however, some start earlier and others end later.

- **Arlington, Va.** Community Garage Sale: North Quincy St. and North 15th St. First Saturday of the month 9 a.m. to 2 p.m. May through November.
- **Gaithersburg, Md.** Flea Market: 31 S. Summit Ave. in the parking lot across from City Hall. Second Saturday of the month 9 a.m. to 2 p.m. May through October.
- **Civitans Flea Market:** Shady Grove Rd. and Redland Rd., Gaithersburg, Md. at the Shady Grove Metro parking garage. Fourth Saturday of the month 7 a.m. to 1 p.m. April through October.
- **Georgetown,** D.C. Flea Market: Rosario Center, Wisconsin Ave. at S St. N.W. Sundays 9 a.m. to 5 p.m. April through December.
- **Vienna, Va.** Flea Market: Nottoway Park, 9601 Courthouse Rd.; various summer months, 9 a.m. to 3 p.m..
- In Maryland, three farmers markets of note

include: **Bethesda Farm Women's Cooperative** (which also has a small flea market): 7155 Wisconsin Ave. Wednesday, Saturday, Sunday 9 a.m. to 5 p.m. through November; **Rockville**, on Middle Lane near the Rockville Metro: Saturdays 9 a.m. to 1 p.m., and Wednesdays 11 a.m. to 2 p.m. June 3 to Oct. 28; and **Bowie** at Bowie High School: 15200 Annapolis Rd. Sunday 9 a.m. to 1 p.m.

Other resources

In addition to local papers, pick up one of the many small papers devoted to antiques, free at many antique stores, for scores of ads and listings of flea markets throughout the mid-Atlantic region. Other resources for the treasure hunter include:

√ Books such as *Collectors' Guide to U.S. Auctions and Flea Markets.* A nationwide listing of hundreds of markets. Available at the library, free; and

√ Listings of farmers markets and pick-your-own produce farms distributed free by local extension services.

Antiques Heaven, Frederick, Maryland

Frederick, Maryland, an exurban city, celebrated its 250th anniversary in 1995. It is home of the minor league baseball team the Frederick Keys (named after notable town citizen Francis Scott Key, who penned our national anthem); land of (it seems) a thousand antique shops; and preserver of historic monuments.

Frugal, friendly Frederick lies beyond Clarksburg and Poolesville, past hilly farmlands and cow pastures northbound on I-270. After you cross from Montgomery County over the Frederick County line, the city is just 10 miles ahead. From Rockville, the trip is about 26 miles. On the way is a free scenic overlook eulogizing the July 9, 1861, Civil War Battle of Monocacy, known as "the battle that saved Washington." It is here that the city's cluster of church spires can be spied for the first time. After this five-minute detour, head for the first Frederick exit off the highway, Market St., Exit 31A, for a direct ride into the historic district.

• Before you go too far, first visit Old Glory Antiques on the outskirts by going past the Francis Scott Key Mall on the right and the Sam's Club on the left, and proceeding about 1 1/2 miles to Old Glory Antiques on the right. Old Glory is a grouping of about 100 antiques vendors within a blue metal-sided building in the parking lot. Open daily, 10-6.

There is a wide range of items here, from sheet music and antique oak dressers to dining room sets, knick-knacks, and household treasures and practical items—all at fairly reasonable prices, especially when compared to similar items found closer to D.C. For example, slag glass from blast furnaces cost 25 cents to $2 (perfect as paperweights or aquarium rocks); ruby red crinkle glass vases for $12; ornately carved oak dining room chair in good condition for $55. The establishment tends to give a 10 percent discount for cash purchases.

• But in terms of antiques, you haven't seen

nothin' yet, as the saying goes, until you've walked down Patrick Street, the heart of Frederick's historic district, where every other townhouse-shop is loaded with what some call antiques and others call secondhand merchandise. A quick survey seemed to indicate, however, that prices in this trendier part of the old town were a bit higher than on the outskirts. For sheer volume of choice, however, this is it.

• There are also several groupings of vendors clustered together here in larger stores, such as Emporium Antiques, which has 130 dealers of what they tout as "an exceptional variety of fine antiques," located at 112 E. Patrick St., open daily.

A wealth of information about the city and events can be obtained at the Visitors' Center off South Market Street at 19 East Church St., phone (301) 663-8687 or (800) 999-3613. Open daily.

For a quick, delicious and frugal lunch, try the Frederick Coffee Co. and Cafe, located in the Everedy Square and Shab Row complex of retail stores and restaurants, within the intersections of Patrick, Wisner, East Church, and East Streets. A big knish with sweet potato chips and green bean chips was just $3; a bowl of vegetarian chili was $3.50. The gourmet coffee of the day was 50 cents for 8 ounces, 80 cents for 10 ounces, or 95 cents for 12 ounces. Homemade muffins at $1.25 and desserts from under $1 are also available along with a multitude of gourmet coffees.

• Proceeding down Market to right on Seventh St., and then left on East St., look for the

Mondo Flea Market store on the right at 712 East Street, open Tuesday through Sunday. The store offers what it calls "an eclectic collection of the old, the cool, and the weird." Here we found lots of extremely tacky old stuff with some serious collectibles. A box of Nixon for President buttons was marked "Lest we forget." A penny holder statuette near the cash register also held this sign: "I am the goddess of financial well-being. Grease my shell." The basement houses a huge collection of secondhand books and magazines.

• Diagonally across the street, we found Quality Consignment Shop, at 801 East St. The owner told us Frederick has five pawnshops, five consignment stores, a used toy store, four Goodwill "select seconds" stores, and about 500 yard sales every year listed in the paper between March and October (she said she had counted last year). Quality Consignment itself was packed with basic, gently worn clothing for people of all ages and genders, toys and baby items, at reasonable prices.

Other unique stores abound in this shoppers' haven. Further back on 420 East Patrick St. across from the Chat 'N Chew restaurant, we found a factory outlet specializing in tall and big men's clothes; they carried few women's clothes.

At 16 North Market St. we saw Country Wares of Frederick, a gift shop devoted to bears and bears and bears (some pigs, cows, and bunnies available, too).

At 13 South Wisner St., is the McCutcheon's Factory Store, producers of fruit products since

1938, including apple butter, fresh apples, preserves, juices, dressings, cider, mustards, relishes, hot sauces, and gift baskets, some at wholesale and some at retail prices.

• Bookworms could lose themselves at Wonder Books and Video, which claims to be the largest used bookstore in the Baltimore-Washington region, at 1306 West Patrick St, open daily; (301) 694-5955.

For overnight stays, Frederick offers about a dozen hotels and motels, many with budget rates. There are also about a dozen bed and breakfast inns. A special side trip can be taken to one of several local wineries, including the Elk Run Vineyard in Mt. Airy (410) 775-2513, or (800) 414-2513.

Among the fine entertainment offerings too numerous to list here, is the Baltimore Symphony Orchestra, which has been playing a series of concerts in the city for 27 years. Write to BSO In Frederick, P.O. Box 453, Frederick Maryland 21705-0453.

The Delaplaine Visual Arts Center, a film enthusiast cooperative "dedicated to the preservation of the film arts through community activism and education" at 40 South Carroll St., sponsors free films throughout the year (301) 698-0656.

For sports enthusiasts, the city's Single A minor league baseball team, the Keys, are a bargain at just $5 for adult general admission, $3 for seniors over 62 and children, and $9 for field box seats (first four rows), and $7 for next for rows of box seats. The season starts in April and season tickets and partial plans are available in advance and during the year. For more information, call the Keys at (301) 662-0013.

Hooray for Frederick, still frugal after all these years!

Community Focuses

Chapter 7

IN THIS CHAPTER, WE TAKE YOU to eight Washington metro area communities: two in Washington; three in suburban Maryland; and two in Virginia. Each community focus strives to give an overall, but by no means comprehensive, tour of some of the best frugal spots in the capital area.

FOGGY BOTTOM, GEORGETOWN, D.C.

Since so many residents of the metro area spend their working days in the downtown D.C. area, we thought it fitting that our first tour should be of well-populated (daily Monday through Friday, anyway) Georgetown. This community "spills over" into Foggy Bottom. We have discovered several little-known thrift shops there that are worth a metro or cab ride from the downtown area (defined as a one-mile radius surrounding Connecticut and K Streets Northwest).

Nearly everyone complains that it is expensive to work downtown, citing the cost of commuting and/or parking, food, and professional clothing. It can be expensive, but it doesn't have to be. Here are suggestions for some of the best buys in the area, guaranteed to keep those professional wardrobe/gotta eat lunch costs down by potentially thousands of dollars per year.

Years of brown-bagging it to work downtown have taught us that one can bring a hearty sandwich (tuna, cheese, whatever), fruit, a drink, chips, etc. from home for about $1 to $1.50 a day, while comparable downtown lunches (the kind you bring back to the office in a bag, not restaurant meals) cost about $5 to $7 per day. That's a savings of at least $70 per month, or $840 per year. Plus, *you* control the quality. How many hours does it take you to earn $840? And that's gross pay, of course, not net.

However, if you have not brought your lunch from home and don't want to spend $3 to $5 just for a deli sandwich, there are several local grocery stores you can go to. But don't expect huge savings on groceries downtown. If you commute from the suburbs, in general you will do much better buying where you live. You also can keep a few "staple items" in your desk at work to supplement from the following grocery stores.

The Townhouse Safeway at the corner of 21st and M Streets caters to the lunchtime crowd, with make-your-own sandwich and salad bars and other pre-cooked foods such as barbequed chicken. You might do better there buying perishables such as yogurt and a piece of fruit, a loaf of bread when you need it, and combine with the tuna or peanut butter that you keep in your desk. (Tip: If you have access to a microwave, Ramen noodles or their generic version with leftover meat and/or vegetables brought from home make a filling quick lunch for under 30 cents).

Federal Market at 23rd Street between M and

N Streets also has a soup and salad bar, and they make sandwiches at the deli counter. The sandwiches are definitely for big eaters. A tuna sandwich will run you $4.69! (Giant's Superdeals section recently sold a four-pack of Bumble Bee solid white Albacore for $4.99, so even the biggest eater would save more by hauling his catch from home.)

Clothing-Conscious Considerations You can spend a fortune on clothes in the downtown/ Georgetown area (or elsewhere, trying to "look professional"), especially if you frequent fancy shops. However, the flipside of the elegant Georgetown stores and their equally tony clientele that few people know about is—the Georgetown area thrift shops! Here you can obtain castoffs of the rich and famous for as little as 5 percent of the original price. Most of these garments are beautifully made, and in good to excellent condition (some even have the original tags on them and have never been worn!). Here are some of the best, from the least expensive to the most:

- The Seller's Door is in the basement of the Church of the Pilgrim at 23rd and P Streets. Its hours are extremely limited: Thursdays and Saturdays from 10 a.m. to 1 p.m. This is one of the best, cheapest places to get clothing and toys for infants and younger kids and casual clothing for adult women (sorry guys; the selection for you is pretty much limited to a few sweaters and a box of ties). This is a no-frills establishment. A lot of times you have to knock on the door so the woman who runs the shop can let you in. Clothing here can include an Adrienne Vittadini hand-knitted multicolored sweater for a toddler for 50 cents; or a 100 percent down vest for an older child for $2. For adults, there are finds like Liz Claiborne sportswear for under $1 apiece. Much of the sportswear is in boxes and has to be sifted through.

- Round Two is another church basement establishment, Christ Church at the corner of 31st and O Streets. Its hours also are limited: 10 a.m. to 3 p.m. each Wednesday. This shop has a good selection of women's clothes and men's clothes, but is more limited for children's. It also has a nice collection of books in the back, most for $1 or less. If you like fine china and glassware, Round Two seems to attract a fair number of pieces of cut glass, china, and other such items. These make nice gifts for collectors, or to fill out a set of one's own from which a few pieces have been lost, at much less than antique store prices. We saw several elegantly dressed gentlemen purchasing these items and saying out loud they were buying them as gifts, this past Christmas. It's a sure bet more than a few Georgetown antique dealers frequent this thrift shop.

- The Thrift Shop at 27th and P Streets N.W. is the repository of both donations (mostly downstairs) and consignments (mostly upstairs) from board members (and their friends and neighbors) from four local hospitals, including Children's Hospital. Hours are 9:30 a.m. to 4:30 p.m. Tuesday through Saturday. This store has a wide selection of merchandise (somewhat limited for children), including women's designer clothes, fancy lingerie, and men's suits. The consignment shop prices are variable; sometimes you can get a very good buy (two hand-quilted brand new sofa pillows for $6 apiece, for example). Much of the time the prices are good buys compared to an antique shop. If an item does not sell within a certain number of months in the consignment shop, the price is marked down. Visa, MasterCard, personal checks accepted.

All of these stores make interesting lunchtime excursions. Sometimes you come away emptyhanded since merchandise turnover makes selection erratic. Often, however, you come away with something practical, and fairly frequently with a real "find."

Miscellaneous Markets Several other Georgetown stores yield especially good buys:

- **Jewelry.** One of the classiest pawn shops you'll ever see is Diener's Jewelers at 1710 M St. N.W. Pawned, unredeemed jewelry can be obtained at very good prices. Clients are said to include Washington lawyers, officials, and other professionals whose lifestyle got a bit overextended. Press a buzzer to be let in. Not much costume jewelry here, but if you're looking for gold and jewels for a Frugal Splurge at a fraction of jewelry store prices, this is a good place.

- **Music and books.** For selection, Tower Records at 2000 Pennsylvania Avenue is hard to beat. Second Story Books, at 2000 P St. has a good selection of secondhand books.

- **Vendors.** Don't pass the street vendors

by, it's not all junk out there. Some of them have overstock of perfumes that sell for many times more in the stores, flower shop rejects that won't last quite as long as the florists' will but are pretty nonetheless; costume jewelry (again sometimes overstock of good-quality costume jewelry such as Monet); and umbrellas on rainy days, warm gloves and hats in season (if you need 'em, you need 'em, and they are cheap).

K Street between Connecticut Ave. and 20th Street is especially thick with vendors, as is the area in front of the Foggy Bottom metro station. The earring vendor at Foggy Bottom sometimes gets imported brass earrings from Thailand, some department store name brand costume jewelry, and we've never seen his prices exceed $2.50 for a pair. (He also sells pantyhose for $1 for harried office workers who "hit a snag" on the way to work).

- **Camping gear.** Not that you need it most days downtown, but when you've got to have a new tarpaulin, de-buggers of the insecticidal kind, or plain sweats or thermals, Sunny's Surplus is the place to go. Here you can buy an inflatable neck pillow for about $3.00; the same kind go for about $10 in specialty stores and department store luggage departments.

So although it could be expensive to work downtown, if you know just a few bargain havens, you can save those greenbacks to spend elsewhere in the capital city.

EASTERN MARKET, CAPITOL HILL, D.C.

Eastern Market is the only historic, fresh food market remaining in Washington, according to the association formed to preserve this community institution. Housed in a brick building constructed in 1873, the market is listed on the National Register of Historic Places.

Eastern Market is located in Capitol Hill's historic district on Seventh St. S.E. between C St. and North Carolina Ave. It is one block north of the Eastern Market metro stop on the Blue and Orange lines. Limited parking can be found on Seventh St. and on the alleys adjoining the market building.

The Fund for Eastern Market, a private, non-profit organization established in 1990, has sponsored a dance series other efforts to raise money for programs and improvements at the market. For more information, phone: (202) 543-0587.

The Fund calls the market "living history," since for more than 100 years, farmers and their families from Maryland, Virginia, and West Virginia have been bringing their fresh produce, baked goods, and flowers there.

Open Saturdays, the market is also renowned for fresh meats, fish, and poultry. The aromas of coffees and pastries and flowers, etc., are enticing, but the fruits and vegetables seemed to be sold at city prices. One vendor offered beautiful Vidalia onions for $1 a pound, for example. But the same onions, in quality and freshness, could be bought the same day at Magruder's in the suburbs for just 50 cents per pound.

Then again, the strawberries, dried fruit and nuts, chili peppers and the like were mostly still in the boxes they arrived in from the farm, and in some cases, still on the truck! And there were bargains to be found amidst the cornucopia-like plenty of the market: fresh cut flowers were often a deal, for example, with sweetheart roses in all colors priced at $4 for six.

The South Hall of the building contains the public food market. The North Hall, designed in a classic revival style by Snowden Ashford and built in 1907, is known as the Market 5 Gallery and operates as an arts and community center. The arts side of the building and the markets surrounding Eastern Market are open Saturday and Sunday 10 a.m. to 5 p.m. March through December. Saturday is for crafts, Sundays is flea market day.

Market 5 Gallery is open Sunday through Friday, 12-5 p.m., and Saturday 10 a.m.-5 p.m. For more information, call (202) 543-7293. The flea market also is a more than a century-old institution.

The crafts market has a variety of media such as photography, sculpture, wood, jewelry, oil and acrylic paintings. But other items, such as antique furniture, imported objects, and what the marketers call good old American junque, can be found as well. Frequent special events include musical entertainment.

One local artist there sold 1950s and 1960s

pots and kitchen utensils turned into clocks in the $32 range. Others offer hand-crafted drums, Mexican silver jewelry at better-than-retail prices, ironwood sculptures, handcrafted picnic baskets, and children's handmade clothing. For more information on the flea market, call Tom Rall, manager, at (703) 534-7612.

Overall, this short, but crowded strip is loaded with unique finds, many under $10, such as the decoupage light switch plates starting at $8, and the Indian tin potpourri boxes at $4.

• While the food and crafts market is the main attraction, there are four fine consignment shops in this one block span that city dwellers must love. Capitol Hill Books at 657 C St. S.E. advertised "good used books bought and sold."

• Another shop is Clothes Encounters of a Second Kind, 202 Seventh St. S.E. Hours: Mon.-Fri. 11 a.m.-6 p.m.; Thurs. until 7 p.m.; Sat. 10 a.m.-6 p.m.; and Sunday 12-4 p.m. A women's store loaded with very stylish, well made outfits, dress gowns, separates, jewelry, and accessories, this shop was packing in the customers while we were there.

• A Man for All Seasons, 321 7th St. S.E., a small, one-dressing room shop, much like a men's boutique clothing store, offered Capitol Hill attire (for example, designer silk ties, and designer sports wear and business suits) for upper level, resale prices. An Eddie Bauer one-pocket button-down shirt was priced at $12, about half of full retail. Hours: Tues.-Fri. 11-6, Thurs. 11-7, Sat. 10-6.

George Washington may not have shopped

Eastern Market, but *we* did, and it was worth the trip!

BETHESDA, MARYLAND

Bethesda, Md., in Montgomery County, has long been known as one of the Washington, D.C. area's nicest and most well-established suburbs.

Like the Georgetown area of northwest D.C., the flip side of Bethesda's high-toned shopping establishments (Saks Fifth Avenue, Mazza Gallerie, etc.) are a slew of consignment shops, as well as long listings in the papers each week of garage and estate sales. In addition, there is a fine farmers market open twice a week, and a low-cost, dine-in movie theater.

Special Shops. Let's start out with the consignment and thrift shops. To get alliterative about it, a large number of such stores are on what we call the Cordell Consignment Corridor. Along Cordell Avenue., off Old Georgetown Road (nearest metro stop is Bethesda or NIH, on the Red Line), one may find a number of "high-end" consignment shops where designer clothes, furniture, and some antiques may be found. The shop owners' standards of acceptance for merchandise are high. Some of the addresses are on Woodmont Ave., a main street which Cordell crosses. One could spend a whole day (and a fair amount of money) if you started early in the morning and combed the Cordell Corridor carefully. Here's a list of several shops in that area, in alphabetical order:

- Cordell Collection Furniture—used and

antique furniture. 4911 Cordell Ave. Hours are Monday, Tuesday, Wednesday, and Friday 10 a.m. to 5 p.m.; Thursday, 10 a.m. to 7 p.m.

• Good After New—furniture, antiques, clothing. 4865 Cordell Ave. Visa and Master Card accepted. Mon-Fri 9 a.m. to 6 p.m., Saturday 9 a.m. to 5 p.m.

• Next to New—4918 St. Elmo Ave., 9:30 a.m. to 5 p.m. Monday through Saturday.

• Second Chance—ladies, children, some designers. 7702 Woodmont Ave. Tuesday through Saturday 10 a.m. to 5 p.m. Sunday 12-4; Monday 12-5.

• The Ritz— 4851 Cordell Ave. 10 a.m. to 5 p.m., Monday through Saturday.

• Think New-4912 Cordell Ave.; Monday through Saturday 10 a.m. to 5 p.m.

• Vintage to Vogue Resale Boutique—8121 Woodmont Ave. Hours Monday through Saturday 10 a.m. to 6 p.m. Tuesday and Thursday, 10 a.m. to 6 p.m.

Thrifty and Cooperative. There are also two thrift shops worth mentioning, where one can donate rather than consign clothes. They are the Montgomery County Thrift Shop, 7125 Wisconsin Ave. (9:30 a.m. to 4:15 p.m. Monday through Saturday), and the Opportunity Shop at 4710 Bethesda Ave., open 10 a.m. to 4 p.m. Tuesday through Saturday.

During late spring and throughout the summer, when the newspapers are chock full of advertisements for yard and estate sales, it seems that the listings for Bethesda are particularly extensive. These are worth looking in on (bring your map so you can find the side streets).

The Bethesda Women's Cooperative on Wisconsin Ave., is open Wednesdays and Saturdays from 7 a.m. to 3 p.m. It features locally produced produce, poultry, meats, etc. Herbs and spices are particularly fresh and especially cheap here. It's definitely worth a trip.

Frugal Flicks. The Bethesda Theater Cafe (formerly the Bethesda Cinema and Drafthouse) 7719 Wisconsin Ave. (call (301) 656-3337 for movie schedules) features recent-run movies, free parking, food, beer and wine. Admission is $3.25 weekdays and Sundays, $4.00 Friday and Saturday.

The Bethesda Theater Cafe, before it was the Drafthouse, was the Bethesda Theater, one of the large, old-style moviehouses that Washington used to have in abundance. Although it's been changed to accommodate the restaurant-style tables, some of that movie palace ambience still lingers. It just has one screen; it did not get turned into a 12-plex or as Jay Leno puts it, "a concrete bunker at the end of the mall." It's informal and a fun place to go, and the food's not bad either.

On a frugalist's excursion to Bethesda, one might consider visiting the women's co-op in the morning (perhaps fortifying one's energy with some of their delicious local low-cost produce), then hit the yard and estate sales, stroll the Cordell Corridor and nearby environs, and finish up with dinner, a beverage, and a movie at the Bethesda Theater Cafe. Sounds like a nice day to us!

BOWIE, MARYLAND

Bowie, Md., an incorporated city of about 40,000 residents, is located about 12 miles from Annapolis, and 15 from the Capitol Building in Washington, D.C., in northern Prince George's County near the Anne Arundel County line.

Bowie was a small community of just a few thousand residents until 1962 when builder William Levitt established the third "Levittown" there. He called this development Belair at Bowie, not Levittown, as he did his first two developments, in respectively, Long Island in New York, and Pennsylvania.

Thirty years after Belair was first built, the community now has a reputation as one of the yard sale meccas of the D.C. area. On any given Saturday morning between March and early November, there are scores of yard sales, some beginning as early as 7 a.m., though most are over by 2 p.m.

Yard sale times tend to vary from community to community throughout the capital area; in some, sales may continue on to 5 p.m. In Bowie, people tend to pack up early so they can get to the beach or the Chesapeake Bay, both of which are as close as they can possibly be to a community that still considers itself part of the D.C. metro area.

Bowie is an extremely family-oriented community, and consequently the yard sales are gold mines for clothes, toys, books and other items for children ranging in age from one week old to teenhood.

The local paper, the *Bowie Blade-News*, which comes out on Thursdays, lists many yard sales, and the ads often give clues as to sizes of clothes, and other details offered. If you're looking to save money on back-to-school items, for example, it is probably worth it to get up early on a Saturday and make the excursion to Bowie. (Beltway east to Route 50—John Hanson Highway; then get off at Route 197, Collington Road and go either north or south. Bowie sprawls, but pick up a copy of the Blade-News at one of the numerous convenience stores to read the ads, and also watch for road signs for unadvertised sales.)

A couple of shops known for their bargains are:

- The American Cancer Society's Discovery Shop thrift shop for Prince George's County, located in Bowie Plaza Shopping Center, Route 197 near Old Chapel Road, 6904 Laurel-Bowie Rd. Hours: Tues., Weds., Fri. 10 a.m.-5:30 p.m.; Thurs 10 a.m.-8 p.m.; Sat. 10 a.m.-4 p.m.

- Down the road in nearby Crofton is K.D.'s Consignments (formerly Mary's Consignments), 2173 Defense Highway, which has a good selection of women's and small children's clothing, some jewelry, vintage clothing, antiques.

- Hilltop Shopping Center, on Route 450 and Racetrack Rd,, has the Outlet Store, a shop open every day except Saturday that carries a good selection of sweats, t-shirts, some socks and lightweight luggage, at extremely competitive prices. Some children's clothing. Hours are Mon.-Thurs. 9:30-9 p.m.; Fri. 9:30-8:30 p.m.; Closed Sat., but open Sun 10-6 p.m.; 6828A Racetrack Rd Hilltop also has a T.J. Maxx discount store.

Between March and October, the City of Bowie sponsors a small but high-quality farmer's market every Sunday from 9 a.m. to 1 p.m. in the parking lot at Bowie High School, Route 450, 15200 Annapolis Rd. For those who like to purchase organic produce, much of the produce here is grown with no pesticides.

The City of Bowie has its own theater, set back in the woods in a park near Routes 450 and 301. There are several local theater groups that put on productions there year-round, all at reasonable prices. Although production values are sometimes amateurish (though also often quite good), the setting is always lovely at the (indoor) Theater in the Woods. Check the local papers' weekend sections for productions, or call Bowie City Hall at (301) 262-6200.

Bowie State University (formerly Bowie State College), one of the older historically African-American colleges, also often features theatrical productions, 14000 Jericho Park Road, (301) 464-3000.

For those who like to go antique-hunting, "Historic Old Bowie" (that's what the sign at the intersection of Routes 197 and 564 says) offers over a dozen shops with prices less expensive than other better-known antiquing communities.

And, of course, for baseball fans, there's the Bowie Baysox and their state-of-the-art-for minor-league baseball stadium. The Baysox are a farm team for the Orioles. Both the stadium (surrounded by trees) and its old-fashioned baseball ambience are getting rave reviews.

TAKOMA PARK, MARYLAND

Takoma Park, Maryland, is a hip, artsy community that used to legally exist in the jurisdictions of two counties, Montgomery and Prince George's County; it is now all part of Montgomery county. It also sits nearly on top of the D.C. line.

On a crisp fall afternoon, these authors started their trek at the end of Carroll Ave. at the Takoma Park Metro station, driving past two funeral homes until the road forked at Willow St., and going straight to stay on Carroll, decidedly the main drag. We found parking on the street right away. (On the way we passed Roland's Unisex Hair Salon, which offered senior citizens' cuts for $5.)

Takoma Park is kind of funky, kind of trendy, kind of laid-back. Many of the places we stopped at did not have their hours posted either on the front door or on a business card, and when we asked, we were often told business hours varied. The first weekend in December is the annual holiday open house for many of the merchants in the old town section on Carroll Ave. and this may be one of the best times to visit.

• The House of Musical Traditions at 7040 Carroll Ave. touts folk instruments, books, and recordings from around the world, and offers information on lessons, concerts, repairs, imports and mail order sales. In addition to fine instruments from $1 nose flutes to the $500 accordians, the store offered its famous $3 flute bin, which contained simple wooden flutes from around the world. It also had sheet music, lots of small and unusual items, and high-quality-sounding wind chimes at reasonable prices. Hours are Tuesday through Friday, 12-7 p.m.; Sat. 11 a.m.-7 p.m., Sun. 11 a.m.-5 p.m. and closed on Mondays.

• About a block away, across the street near the old town clock (which tells us 1883 was the time in which the community was founded), in the 6900 block we found Takoma Old Town Antiques and Collectibles. The only hours posted were Saturdays 10 a.m.-4 p.m., and the owner said these were still tentative. Next door at 6923 Carroll Ave. was the Everyday Gourmet, a sit-down deli that offered many unique food items and fresh baked treats, but not necessarily at what we would consider everyday prices. Hours are Mon.-Fri. 8 a.m.-8 p.m.; Sat. 10 a.m.-5 p.m.; Sun. 10-3 p.m.

Back in the car and driving to the next locale, we veered to the left where Carroll meets Sycamore Ave. and Ethan Allen Ave. to stay on Carroll. A row of townhouse style shops and services signaled us that this must be the place for frugalists.

• On the corner behind a laundromat, is the classy Honorable Mention women's clothing consignment boutique at 7334 Carroll Ave.. From the fur-trimmed suit that stood at attention on the Colonial-style porch at the entrance on Lee Ave., to the like-new jewelry case, this clothing consignment shop had it all. A small space jammed with high quality labels such as Saks Fifth Ave., Yves St. Laurent, and others. But the prices were fabulous. A small, wicker $1 box in the back room contained various items from dresses to purses. A row of stunning and sophisticated evening gowns seemed fairly priced. Hours are Sat.-Sun 1p.m.-6 p.m.

• A couple of doors down was Knee High to a Grasshopper, a children's consignment store, at 7326 Carroll Ave. About half of the merchandise here appeared to be brand new, many of the items unusual or special, most high quality and some pricey. Quick mittens with velcro closings down the sides to make it easy to put on or take off a child were priced at $6.99. Hours: Mon.-Sat. 10-6, Sun. 12-4.

• Not much further was Takoma Picture Framers at 7312 Carroll Ave., a mixture of custom-made frames and secondhand collectibles. It had many glass items. We enjoyed the prints for 10 cents, the basket of tins for $1 each, greeting cards for 5 cents, and some (but not as many as you would expect) photo frames ranging from $6 to $20.

• We drove back to the three-way split, this time turning left onto Ethan Allen, which we followed until we reached New Hampshire Ave., where we turned left. Following New Hampshire about 2 miles, we ventured into the Salvation Army Thrift Store, a gigantic department store of thrift, at 7505 New Hampshire Ave., #202. The merchandise varied nicely in style, type, and sizes, but because it is a thrift store, was generally less gently used than consignment shop items. The store's large collection of baskets and books was notable.

- The Caribbean Market just below Salvation Army in the same plaza was a find for spice lovers. Hard-to-find saffron was just $1.89 for three ounces. Jamaican curry cost $5.54 for 22 ounces. (The local Safeway's Crown Colony brand of curry costs $2.19 for 1.3 ounces.) But here ground coriander was 99 cents for six ounces (compared to McCormick at Safeway at $3.49 for 1.25 ounces).

- The final stop was the Goodwill Shop about a mile further, 8016 New Hampshire Ave., in the Sassafras-Dollar Store strip plaza. This was even better organized than Salvation Army, and at first glance appeared to be a retail store.

No doubt about it, the shopping in Takoma Park is an interesting mixed bag.

LAUREL, MARYLAND

This community of about 20,000 people in Prince George's County, is the mailing address for more than 64,000 people altogether, who are located in Howard and Anne Arundel counties, as well as Prince George's.

Easily accessible by Interstate 295 (the Baltimore-Washington Parkway) and Interstate 95, the town is a half-hour-to-forty-five minute drive from

Washington, D.C. and Baltimore.

Laurel's Main Street, bounded by U.S. Route 1 and I-95, has been designated a historic district. It has a variety of antique and arts and crafts shops, as well as late-Victorian-era homes.

Another building of historic interest is the town's 18th-century Montpelier Mansion, located on Route 197 near the Baltimore-Washington Parkway entrance. The Montpelier Cultural Arts Center (301-953-1993) is a large building built in 1979 on the mansion's grounds at Route 197 and Muirkirk Road that often hosts low-cost or no-cost cultural events, such as concerts or art exhibitions.

The center is operated by the Maryland-National Capital Park and Planning Commission. Inside the arts center, there are three large galleries, classrooms, and studios where about 21 resident artists rent space. It is open to the public seven days a week from 10 a.m. to 5 p.m., and visitors can see the artists and their works, which include painting, pottery, and photography, among others.

Cultural Attractions. Another home-grown cultural attraction in Laurel is the Laurel Oratorio Society, which is more than 25 years young. The group does four performances each year: two classical concerts with orchestra and two lighter shows featuring popular music or show tunes. The oratorio group, has been known, together with the Prince George's Philharmonic and the National Ballet of Maryland to occasionally mount superb productions, such as Carl Orff's "Carmina Burana," at local high schools, for incredibly low admission prices.

Another plus in the Laurel area for musical buffs is the U.S. Army Field Band and its component musical groups—the Jazz Ambassadors, Concert Band, chamber ensembles, etc., which present free concerts at Fort Meade, off Route 198, that are open to the public (301-677-6231).

The Patuxent Environmental Science Center off Route 197 south of Laurel touts a newly opened National Wildlife Visitor Center (301-497-5760) off Powder Mill Road just west of Route 197, featuring interactive exhibits on wildlife and environmental issues. It also has an extensive trail system and outdoor education sites for school classes. It is open daily from 10 a.m. to 5 p.m. The North Tract Visitor Contact Station (410-674-3304) off Route 198 just west of Route 32, offers guided bird and butterfly walks, owl prowls and other educational seminars throughout the year.

Antiques, Thrift. As frugalists well know, where there are antique stores, there are thrift and consignment stores, too. Laurel, with its "Antique Alley" on Main Street, is no exception.

- A particular favorite thrift store is the Village Thrift Store at 9644 Fort Meade Road (Route 198). The store, open seven days a week, is large and carries a wide range of merchandise, from clothes to furniture to books to jewelry. Merchandise is labeled with different-colored cardboard tags, three colors of which are chosen daily to be half-price merchandise. This particular shop has yielded some truly treasurable finds, including a Stone Mountain brand leather purse in excellent condition, for 45 cents, a handmade American quilt from the 1940s in an "around the world" pattern for $25, a handmade lace and cotton baby quilt for $1.90, and a child's Redskins satin jacket in perfect condition for $6.40. The merchandise is priced rather arbitrarily (some things are actually overpriced), but this place definitely is worth traveling to and exploring.

Other thrift and consignment shops in Laurel include:

- Amvets Thrift Store, 988 South Baltimore Rd. and the Ft. Meade Thrift Store at Ernie Pyle & Lewellyn Streets at Ft. Meade (the latter is for military personnel only).
- Select Seconds Consignment Boutique, 418 Main St.
- Something Old Something New Bridal Consignment shop (301-490-6642; by appointment only).
- Play It Again Sports at 14130 Baltimore Ave.

The town sports a range of restaurants, from fast food to fairly pricey. Our favorites include the Tastee Diner (a real old-style diner that's been around for years), at 118 Washington Blvd. where entrees range from $3 to $9; and Red Hot & Blue for barbeque at 677 Main Street.

On a national basis, Laurel is perhaps most famous for its racetrack, but as frugalists we can't exactly recommend going there as a way to save money.

All in all, Laurel gets laurels from us.

ALEXANDRIA, VIRGINIA

Six miles south of Washington on the west bank of the Potomac River, Alexandria, Va. harbors historic structures and relics that date back to before the signing of the Constitution.

But Old Town, as the city's historic district is known, also gives new life to older (though by no means ancient) and more practical artifacts of daily life, such as clothes and household goods, through a respectable number of resale, thrift and consignment stores. One will also discover there several inexpensive, but quality restaurants and entertainment venues.

To get there, take Metro by the Yellow and Blue Lines to the King St. station. From there, walk (about 20 minutes or 15 blocks), catch a cab (about $5) or take the city's DASH bus for 75 cents (which leaves every 20 minutes) to the Visitor's Center at 221 King St. (703) 838-4200, in the center of Old Town. Here you can get maps, general information, listings of restaurants and consignment shops, and a place to use the restroom, all for free. If you drive, you can obtain a 24-hour parking pass. Open daily except on major holidays.

From there, you can go toward the waterfront and the historic Torpedo Factory Arts Center, at 105 N. Union St., 838-4565, where munitions were produced for World War I and World War II. The building now houses an art center with free admission for its ever-changing exhibitions.

For a donation of your choosing, you can take an afternoon tour between 12-5 of the tall ship Schooner Alexandria docked at Waterfront Park between King and Prince Streets; 549-7078.

Or, you can start walking back up King St. toward the metro. Behind the city hall and its beautiful fountains, at 405 Cameron St. (across from Gadsby's Tavern), is the non-profit consignment shop for the Elder Crafters of Alexandria, a gift shop with handcrafted items made by seniors over 55. Open Tues-Sat 10-4; (703) 683-4338.

The number of consignment shops in Alexandria is far beyond the number listed below, but we stayed within the historic district.

- Back on King St. at 821, is Second Glance, a pricey but elegant women's clothing consignment shop.
- Across the street is the Selfhelp Crafts of the World shop, at 824 King St.; 684-1435. Unique and often reasonably priced items could be found here from Filipino finger puppets at $2.75 to jewelry, baskets, toys, textiles, and coffees.
- Cross the street the other way to 900 King St. and you've arrived at one of the all-time classic thrift shops, Prevention of Blindness Thrift; 683-2558. This is a place to find buried treasure, or at least a nice candlestick, or a chuckle over the store's policies. For example: "No exchanges. No layaways. No Refunds. No change given without purchase. Books are priced according to whim." Women's and men's clothing items were priced

from $3; small appliances started at $4; and suitcases at $5. Hours are Tues-Sat 12-7; Sun 12-5; closed Monday.

One good place to find a reasonably priced place to eat is the vicinity of King St. and North Washington. Several chain restaurants and fast food establishments prevail, but these can be tailored to more frugal tastes. At the Grind and Brew Cafe, for example, at 631 King St. A Snaks Fifth Avenue sandwich of ham and Swiss cheese on a crunchy roll was $3.70 for lunch.

- A little farther up the road, at 106 1/2 N. Columbus St. is Funk N Junk; 836-0749. This 1950s retro hole-in-the-wall is jam-packed mostly with goofy household stuff from the era of poodle skirts and cat-eye glasses. In between are nearly-antique items from early 20th Century America; Hollywood memorabilia; and what seemed like a lot of Barbies and Pee Wee Herman dolls.

- Next door at 106 N. Columbus is the Twig Thrift Shop, primarily clothing, which closes during the month of August; 683-5544.

- By the time you get to Le Melange at 1020 King St., a ritzy women's resale clothing store, 548-4448, you will have trekked past scores of antique shops. They primarily appear to offer for sale very tony furniture and home accessories, much of it in the classic early American tradition.

On Saturday mornings 5-9 there is a free farmers market at 301 King St. Also in the fall there is usually one Saturday devoted to a community yard sale at the Lyceum, the city's history museum at

201 South Washington St., sponsored by the city's local museum groups. The museum itself is open daily except on major holidays. Admission is free.

Another freebie, near the King St. metro is the George Washington Masonic National Memorial, which is open daily, except holidays, and offers tours.

While the retail shopping on Alexandria's King St. is stunning in its sheer volume and variety, the resale sector proved to be accessible and bargain-friendly.

ARLINGTON, VIRGINIA

An established Washington suburb, Arlington, Virginia, is sometimes considered the less-affluent, more commuter friendly neighbor of tony Alexandria. Yet, near the rows of brick colonials and graciously tree-lined streets of its residential neighborhoods are some wonderful resale shops, containing treasures that would be welcome in the most elegant of homes.

A Saturday afternoon excursion can use the following route. From Maryland, take the beltway, 495, to Exit 12A, which is 66 East. Take 66 East to exit 23 West, Washington Blvd.-Lee Highway. At the off-ramp light, follow signs to Washington Blvd.

Almost immediately you will find yourself surrounded by yard sale signs posted on telephone poles along neighborhood streets. But the real reason to come are the renowned resale store bargains. And within about a two-mile radius, you will locate a variety of thrift and consignment shops containing everything from antique furniture to children's clothes.

• Just a short mile or so from the Exit 23 off-ramp, we found the Westover Thrift Shop, 5906 North Washington Blvd. This establishment was chock full of a wide range of interesting items in addition to the usual thrift fare. These included rolls of wallpaper for $5 each; a box of old photographs in good shape labeled "instant relatives" for 50 cents; and ornately carved Victorian styled hardwood easels.

Westover also had a good selection of clothes in all sizes for men, women, and children. Prices here were slightly on the high-end for thrift shops, but lower than many area consignment stores. There were designer labels such as Oleg Cassini and Calvin Klein, and better maternity wear such as Peas in a Pod, all in the $15 to $35 range, with less fancy names priced even lower. This fairly large store has old and new furniture, bedding, and jewelry. Hours are 10 a.m. to 6 p.m. Mon.-Sat.

• After leaving Westover, we continued on Washington Blvd. past Swanson Middle School to Wilson Blvd., next to the Clarendon Metro Station. Although closed, the Flea Market Store at 3200 Wilson Blvd., a mustard colored building at the corner of Wilson, Fairfax Drive and Irving St., had a sign posted saying it would reopen. From the outside, its multi-paned windows framed gobs of stuff that could be found at any flea market.

A relatively inexpensive lunch can be had

nearby at the Hard Times Cafe, easily a three-star chili parlor, 3028 Wilson Blvd. For $4.95, you can get a large bowl of chili with corn bread or a beef chili dog with cheddar cheese and chopped onions. The restaurant also offers chicken and burger dishes, and boasts beers of the week. A note of caution: WATCH WHERE YOU PARK, on any day of the week, including Saturdays. Several private parking lots in the area have so-called vicious towing policies, as a sign on the door of the Hard Times Cafe put it. We saw several cars being towed.

A cluster of shops at the corner of North Pershing Drive and Washington Blvd. proved to be especially fruitful for resale shopping, and could constitute the center of any frugalist's excursion to Arlington.

- Starting at the end and working over, the first stop was Consignments Unlimited, 2645 N. Pershing Dr. This skinny store was crammed with clothing, jewelry, housewares, some antiques, and a variety of miscellaneous items from compact discs to coasters. Hours are Tues.-Sat. 11 a.m. to 6 p.m. and Sunday 12-5 p.m.

- Next in line was Second Childhood, a well-organized consignment clothing shop serving tots to teens and offering maternity wear as well. Hours are Tues.-Sat. 10 a.m.-5:30 p.m.; Thurs. 12-7:30 p.m.

- Corner Cupboard, 2649 N. Pershing Dr., which touts itself as a store for the creative shopper, occupies the majority of space on this strip of shops. Antique and more recent vintage furniture was especially plentiful as was glassware, including carnival and depression glass; embroidered linens; and collectibles. Same hours as Consignments Unlimited.

- Across the street and one block down, is Book Ends at 2710 N. Washington Blvd., a cozy used-and-rare book store. Its ambience reminds one of similar establishments in New York or Boston, where book lovers congregate to appreciate what the owners call "previously read books."
- Another shop worth mentioning is the Goodwill Store on Arlington Blvd.

All in all, Arlington proved to be a bargain basket for shoppers with frugality on their minds.

And all in all, the national capital area is loaded with more stores and frugal finds than one book can hold. We hope these mini-trips will help take you toward even greater frugal paths. And should you have frugal forays you would like to share, please contact us, and we may include your suggestion in our next guide. Send suggestions to: Capital Frugalist Press, 16010 Pennsbury Drive, Bowie, Maryland 20716

Appendix

Shirley's Consignments
Distinctive Resales
14834 Build America Dr.
Woodbridge, VA 22191
(703) 491-6159

Contract No. _____

Shirley's Consignments is a shop designed for the sale of high quality used and new clothing, small household articles, gift items and selected crafts. Quality is our goal ... good merchandise presented in good condition at bargain prices. We strive for happy buyers and happy consignors. Thank you for your cooperation in helping us maintain our standards.

Consignment Contract

1. Items are accepted on consignment for a period of **45 days**. At the end of the consignment period the consignor will receive **50% of the total sales.**
2. **A service charge of $10.00** is due annually beginning with the first consignment.
3. After we have priced your items the computer will add a handling charge of $1.00 per item. This charge is paid by the consumer and has no effect on the amount you will receive.
4. The shop sets prices on consigned items. Prices are automatically reduced by 20% after the first 30 days of the contract. All items are subject to occassional discount due to store sales, coupons, special events, and promotions.
5. After the 45 day contract period, consignors must pick up any unsold items within 5 days. **On the 50th day items become shop property.**
6. If the consignor plans to pick up any items, they must come in at least one hour prior to closing. **It is the consignor's responsibility to locate their items.** Please bring a bag to carry withdrawn items.
7. Checks are available after the second Friday following the end of the contract period and must be picked up at the store by the consignor. Checks are void 60 days after issue. If a consignor's share totals less than $20.00, the payment will be made in cash. No payments will be given before the end of the contract period.
8. **Shirley's Consignments may not be held responsible for loss or damage to any article for any reason whatsoever.**
9. **Shirley's Consignments** reserves the right to update the contract as the need arises.

Shop Policies

1. **All consignors need an appointment.** After the initial consignment, drop-off appointments can be made.
2. **A limit of 20 items will be accepted with each appointment. Shirley's Consignments** will not go through more than 25 items regardless of the number of items we accept. Items must total at least $50.00.
3. All articles must be of good quality and in very good condition. *Clothing must be freshly washed and ironed or dry-cleaned, and brought in on hangers ready for resale. They must be in style (not over 3 years old), in season and have no stains or be in need of repair. Household items must be attractive, clean and polished if appropriate; batteries or light bulbs must be provided.
4. All items must have a resale value of not less than $3.50 each.
5. Please do not inquire about your consignment until the end of the consignment period. The shop has many consignors, and this has proven to be very time consuming. It is best to check the contract when coming in to pick up unsold items. Please bring your consignment inventory when you come in.

I have read, understand and accept the terms of **Shirley's Consignments** Contract and Shop Policies.

Signature _____ Date _____ SC Rep. _____

Seasonal Guidelines for Consignments

Spring (15 January - 14 April):

Jeans, short and long sleeved blouses and dresses; unlined coats and jackets, cardigans and cotton pullovers; First Communion dresses; drapes and linens.

Summer (15 April - 14 July):

Jeans, shorts, bathing suits; light colors and fabrics; short sleeve and sleeveless blouses and dresses; Prom gowns; drapes and linens.

Fall (15 July - 14 October):

Jeans, dark colored cottons and blends; unlined wool (best in September) short and long sleeved blouses and dresses; cardigans, cotton pullovers; unlined jackets and coats; Formals; drapes and linens. Children's "back-to-school" clothing sells well in August. Scout Uniforms, Tap Shoes. No turtlenecks.

Winter (15 October - 14 January):

Jeans, lined and unlined woolens, long sleeved blouses and dresses; turtlenecks; lined coats and jackets; boots, furs, snowsuits and warm bedding. No drapes or linens. All Christmas items must be in by Dec. 10.

Throughout the Year:

Maternity clothing (in the appropriate season); jewelry; Accessories (scarves, handbags, etc.) Shoes (in like-new condition); baby furniture and equipment; toys, games and childrens books; household items; knickknacks and decorator items.

* Dry cleaning: Items need to be dry cleaned. Washable items need to be laundered between now and your appointment and on hangers. We will return your hangers as we use our own. **We will not accept items with smoke, moth balls or storage odors.** We inspect your items very carefully, it will help us if this is done before your appointment. Check collar for ring-a-round, this happens when items have been hanging for awhile. Remember this is a partnership and quality is our goal. Ask yourself "Would I spend my hard earned money on this item?" Did I purchase this item over three years ago?

Reprinted with permission of Shirley Cohrs

Index

A

Advertising
  Antiques and collectibles, 117
  Classified, *see* Classified ads
  Price matching policies, 47-50
Alexandria, Va.
  Community Focus, 157-160
  Consignment and thrift stores
    AmVets and Goodwill, 57
    Antiques and collectibles, 158-159
    Books, 119
    Clothing, 34
    Furniture, 56
    General, 158-159
    Music CDs and tapes, 111
  Consumer Affairs Administrator, 60
  George Washington Masonic National Memorial, 160
  Greeting card outlet, 107
  Library system, 88
  Tall ship, Schooner Alexandria, 158
AmVets Thrift Stores, locations, 56-57
Annandale, Va., used book store, 120
Antiques
  Advertising memorabilia, 117
  Alexandria, Va., 159
  Books, *see* Books
  Bowie, Md., 149
  Frederick, Md., 129-131
  Guides, 124-126
  Laurel, Md., 155
  Romantic gift ideas, 100-101
Apparel, *See* Clothing
Archaeological digs, St. Mary's County, Md., 86
Arlington, Va.
  Community Focus, 160-163
  Community garage sale, 128

Arlington (Continued)
  Consignment and thrift stores
    Books, 120
    Clothing, 34
    Furniture, 57-58
    General, 161-163
Arlington County
  Library system, 88
  Towns in, *see specific town name*
Art
  Montpelier Cultural Arts Center, 154
  Romantic excursion, 100
  Tharp collection, 126
  Torpedo Factory, 157
Arts and entertainment
  Dance, *see* Dance
  Grass-roots support, 91-92
  Movies, *see* Film
  Music, *see* Music
  Painting and sculpture, *see* Art
  Plays and musicals, *see* Theater
Automobiles, British Embassy listings, 123-124

B

Baileys Crossroads, Va., bakery thrift store, 17
Bakeries, 16-17
Bar code scanners, FTC warning, 17
Baseball
  Bowie Baysox, 150
  Frederick Keys, 133
  Theme week for kids, 86
Bealeton, Va., Flying Circus, 81
Beaver Heights, Md., bakery thrift store, 17
Beltsville, Md., bakery thrift store, 17
Bethesda, Md.
  Bethesda Farm Women's Cooperative, 129
  Community Focus, 144-146
  Consignment and thrift stores
    Baked goods, 17
    Books, 119
    Clothing, 32
    Cordell Corridor, 144-146
    Furniture, 57
  Farmers Market, 129
  Theater Cafe, 146
Better Business Bureau of Metropolitan Washington, 60
Books
  Annual sales, 108
  Buying to resell, 121-122

Collecting, 118-122
Condition of, 118
Depression-era cookbook, 18-20
Library of Congress for values, 125
Library systems, 87-88
Library theme week for children, 84-85
Mildew on, 119
Used book sellers, listing, 119-121; 133
Bowie, Md.
   Antiques in Old Bowie, 149
   Baysox Baseball, 86; 150
   Community Focus, 147-150
   Consignment and thrift stores, 148-149
   Farmers Market, 129; 149
   Freeway Airport, 81
   Yard sales, 147-148
Bridal wear, 37-41
British Embassy resale list, 122-124
Brown-bag savings, 136
Burke, Va., consignment and thrift stores, 33
Bus to Potomac Mills, 25-26

C

Camp Springs, Md., consignment and thrift stores, 32
Camping equipment, 140
Capitol Hill, Community Focus, 141-143
Cars, British Embassy listings, 123-124
Centreville, Va., used book store, 121
Chantilly, Va., greeting card outlet, 107
Children
   Activities, 80-88
   Back-to-school strategies, 74-77
   Birth congratulations from White House, 105
   Diapers, 77-80
   Gifts, 111-112
   Semi-annual sales, 35-36
   Theme activity weeks, 80-87
   Toys, resale stores, 71-74
Classified ads
   British Embassy, 122-124
   Valentines and other personal messages, 100
   Wedding gowns, 38
Clothing
   Children, 73-74
   Cleaning
      Fine washables, 36
      Stain removal, 24

Clothing (continued)
    Consignment stores, 26-39; 44
    Larger sizes for women, 45
    Maternity, 41-45

    Outlet shopping at Potomac Mills, 25-26
    Resale shopping tips, 22-24
    Values, consignment vs. retail, survey, 21
    Wedding gowns, 37-41
    Women's work outfits, cost survey, 21
Collectibles
    Antiques, *see* Antiques
    Books, 118-122
    Definition, 116
    What to collect, 115-116
    What's hot, 120
College Park, Md., airport and museum, 82-83
College theater and music productions, 90-93
Composting, 63-64
Concerts, *See* Music
Consignment stores
    Books, 119-121
    Clothing
        Bridal, 38-39
        Children's, 73-74
        Listings, 28-35
        Maternity, 44
    Community Focus, 130-163
    Contract, sample, 165
    Furniture, 56-58
    Music CDs and tapes, 110-111
    Sports equipment, 71-73
    Tips for shopping resale, 22-24
    Toys, 71-74
    Values survey, consignment vs. retail, 21
Consumer Credit Counseling Service of Greater Washington, 61
Consumer Federation of America, 61
Consumer Product Safety Commission, U.S., 62
Consumers Union of the United States, 61
Cost pyramid, 54-55
Coupons, food
    Consumer savings, 6
    Strategies, 3-4
Crafts
    Activity week for children, 85
    Gift ideas, 100
    Montgomery County Fair, 94

Credit counseling
  Consumer Credit Counseling Service of Greater Washington, 61
  University of Maryland Cooperative Extension Service, 61-62
Crofton, Md. consignments, 148

D
Dale City, Va., Potomac Mills Outlet Mall, 25-26
Dance performances
  College productions, 90-93
  Ticket tips, 89-90
Diapers, 77-80
Dish soap for fine washables, 36
District of Columbia, *See* Washington, D.C.

E
Eastern Market, Community Focus, 141-143
Ellicott City, Md., Railroad Station Museum, 83
Energy costs, *See* Utilities
Entertainment
  Dance, *see* Dance
  Grass-roots support, 91-92
  Movies, *see* Film

Music, *see* Music
Painting and sculpture, *see* Art
Plays and musicals, *see* Theater
Ethnic markets, 11
Examples of savings
  Book resale, 121-122
  Chinese food, 2
  Corn flakes, 4
  Diapers, 78-80
  Dish soap for fine washables, 36
  Lunches at work, 136
  Mini-blinds, 47-48
  Oatmeal, 11
  Orange juice, 4
  Potatoes, 5
  Price matching policies, 47-49

F
Factory outlets
  Bakery thrift stores, 16-17
  Greeting card stores, 107
  Potomac Mills Mall, Dale City, Va., 25-26
Fairfax, Va.
  Bridal rentals, 41
  Consignment and thrift stores
    Books, 120

Fairfax, Va. (Continued)
    Clothing and accessories, 33-34
    Music CDs and tapes, 110
    Library system, 88
Fairfax County
    Consumer Affairs Department, 61
    Library system, 88
    Towns in, *see specific town name*
Falls Church, Va.
    Consignment and thrift stores
        Clothing, 33
        Furniture, 57-58
        Music CDs and tapes, 110
    Library system, 88
Farmers markets
    Maryland, 128-129
    Staples and spices, 11
Film
    Bethesda Theater Cafe, 146
    Big screen for 99 cents, 94
    Delaplaine Visual Arts Center, 133
Flea markets, 126-129
Flowers
    Eastern Market, D.C., 142
    Hairspray hint, 102
    Street vendors, 102
    Valentine's Day, 98-102
Foggy Bottom, D.C., Community Focus, 135-140
Food
    Advance preparation, 12-13
    Back-to-school strategies, 76
    Bethesda Theater Cafe, 146
    Candy as a gift, 102
    Caribbean Market, 153
    Coupons
        Consumer savings, 6
        Strategies, 3-4
    Depression-era cookbook, 18-20
    Eastern Market, D.C., fresh food market, 141-142
    Eating out, survey of reasons, 1
    Farmers markets
        Maryland, 128-129
        Staples and spices, 11
    Grocery industry revenues data, 6
    Growing, *see* Gardening
    Handling and storage, 9
    Heart-shaped cake, 99
    Holidays, 11

Food (Continued)
  Impulse buying trap, 6
  Leftovers, 14-15
  Lunches at work, 136
  Major store chains, 6-12
    Bakery outlets, 16-17
    Incentives, 10
    Price comparisons, 11; 79
  Oatmeal, 11
  Oven/stove efficiency, 13-14
  Packaging, 20
  Pointers, 12-16
  Safety, USDA hotline, 9
  Sales cycles, 3
  Scanners, FTC warning, 17
  Shopping strategies, 2
    Annual savings using, 12
  Stock-up principle, 3
  Unit pricing, 5; 11
Forestville, Md., music CDs and tapes, 110
Frederick, Md.
  Antiques, 129-131
  Baltimore Symphony Orchestra, 133
  Consignment and thrift stores, 132
  Frugal getaway, profile, 129-134

Keys baseball, 86; 133
Furniture
  Resale store listings, 56-58
  Style considerations, 53-54

G

Gaithersburg, Md.
  Consignment and thrift stores
    Clothing, 30
    Sports equipment, 72-73
    Toys, 72
  Flea markets, 128
  Greeting card outlet, 107
Garage sales, *See* Yard sales
Gardening
  Composting, 63-64
  Conservation, 62
  Garden Resources of Washington (GROW), 61
  Information sources, 62-64
  Lawn care services, 67
  Mail order plant catalogs, 66

Gardening (Continued)
   Metaphor for life, 62
   Mulch, 64-65
   Theme week for kids, 85
   Watering costs and tips, 67-70
Georgetown, D.C., Community Focus, 135-140
Gifts
   Baskets, 102
   Catalogs for ideas and prices, 109
   Children, 111-112
   Mall-avoidance tips, 112-113
   Personalized, 108
   Strategy for year-round shopping, 107-109
   Valentine's Day, 98-102
   Wrapping ideas, 113-114
Goddard Space Flight Center, 81
Goodwill Stores, locations, 57
Greeting cards
   Secondhand but never used, 105-106
   White House program, 105
Grocery costs and ideas, *See* Food

H

Health
   Fitness equipment, resale stores, 71-73
   Food handling, 9
Herndon, Va., consignment and thrift stores, 33-34
Holidays
   Food savings, 11
   Gifts for, *see* Gifts
   President's Day, 103-105
   Valentine's Day, 98-102
Home maintenance
   Fabric cleaning tips, 24; 36
   Furniture, 53-58
   Lawn and garden, *see* Gardening
   Paint, 54
   Price matching policies, 47-50

I

Information sources
   Consumer aid, 60-62
   Farmers markets, 129
   Flea markets, 128
   Food storage and handling, 9
   Gardening, 62-63
   "Great Catalog Guide" from DMA, 109
   Library of Congress, 125

Parks, listing, 95-98

K

Kensington, Md., consignment and thrift stores
  Children's clothing, 73
  Collectibles, 56

L

Laurel, Md.
  Antique Alley, 155
  Community Focus, 153-156
  Consignment and thrift stores
    AmVets thrift store, 57
    Bridal wear, 39
    General, 155-156
    Sports equipment, 72
  Greeting care outlet, 107
  Patuxent Environmental Science Center, 155
Lawn care, *See* Gardening
Libraries, 87-88
Library of Congress, 125
Lighting costs, 58-59
Lincoln Memorial, 104
Lists
  Book sellers, used, 119-121; 133
  British Embassy resale items, 122-124
  Consignment and thrift stores, *see* Consignment stores
  Flea markets, 128-129
  Parks and Nature Centers, 95-98
Loudoun County
  Library system, 88
  Towns in, *see specific town name*
Loveville, Md., postmark for Valentine's Day, 101

M

Mail, *See* Postal services
Mall-avoidance tips, 112-113
Manassas, Va., used book store, 121
Maryland *See also specific city, county, or town*
  Attorney General's Consumer Protection Office, 61
  University of Maryland Cooperative Extension Service, 61-62
Maternity clothing, 41-45
Montgomery County
  Composting bins, 63-64
  Consumer Affairs Office, 61
  Fair, crafts at, 94
  Library system, 87

Mulch service, 64-65
Towns in, *see specific town name*
Movies, *See* Film
Moving sales, *See* Yard sales
Mt. Vernon, Va.
 George Washington home, 104
 Greeting card outlet, 107
Music
 Baltimore Symphony Orchestra in Frederick, Md., 133
 CDs and tapes, 109-111
 Community orchestras, 92-93
 House of Musical Traditions, 151
 Laurel Oratorio Society, 154
 Military bands, 84; 90; 93; 155
 Theme week for kids, 84
 University ensembles, 90-93

N
National Arboretum, 63; 98
Nature centers
 Listing, 95-98
 Rock Creek Nature Center, 83
Negotiating with price matching policies, 50
Nottoway Park Flea Market, Vienna, Va., 128

O
Oatmeal, 11
Olney, Md., bridal rentals, 40
Outlets, *see* Factory outlets

P
Paint, 54
Painting and sculpture, *See* Art
Papering the theater audience, 90-91
Parks, 83; 95-98
Patuxent Environmental Science Center, 155
Penn Station, Md., greeting card outlet, 107
Physical examinations for back-to-school, 74
Planes, 81-83
Postal services
 Gift catalogs, 109
 Loveville, Md. postmark, 101
 Plant catalogs, 66
 Two-day frugality, 101
President's Day, 103-105
Price matching policies
 Description, 47-48

Pros and cons, 49-51
Sample policies, 51-53
Savings example: mini-
blinds, 47-48
Tips for using, 49
Price scanners, FTC warning, 17
Prince George's County
Citizens and Consumer Affairs Office, 61
Library system, 87
Towns in, *see specific town name*
Prince William County
Library system, 88
Towns in, *see specific town name*
Pyramid of prices, 54-55

Q
Quilts, 117
Quotations
California billboards of the '70s, 70
Franklin, Benjamin, 119
Grant, Ulysses S., 103
Jefferson, Thomas, 103
Leno, Jay, 146
Roosevelt, Franklin D., 19
Stypeck, Allan, 118
"The Gardener's Catalogue," 62; 67

R
Railroad Station Museum, Ellicott City, Md., 83
Remanufacturing, 59
Rentals
Gardening equipment, 66-67
Wedding apparel, 37-38; 40-41
Resources, *See* Information sources
Reston, Va.
Consignment store, children's, 74
Zoo, children's activity, 85
Rock Creek Nature Center, 83
Rockville, Md.
Bakery thrift stores, 16
Consignment and thrift stores
Books, 119-121
Bridal, 39
Clothing, 30; 32
General, 57-58
Music CDs and tapes, 111
Farmers market, 129
Roses, 98-102

S
Savings examples, *See*

Washington Frugal Mania 177

Examples of savings
School routines, 74-77
Schooner Alexandria, tall ship, 158
Seat Pleasant, Md., AmVets thrift store, 56-57
Signs of the Frugal Times
   Congressional yard sale, 60
   Conservation, 59
   Coupons, 6
   Exercise equipment resale, 73
   Impulse-buying, groceries, 6
   Nordstrom's "recycled" clothing, 35
   Postal Service two-day delivery, 101
   Remanufacturing, 59
Silver Spring, Md., consignment and thrift stores
   Baked goods, 16
   Clothing, 31
   Music CDs and tapes, 111
   Toys, 72
Sports equipment
   Resale stores, 71-73
   Sign of the Frugal Times, 73
Springfield, Va., consignment and thrift stores
   Books, 120
   Bridal clothing, 40
   Clothing, 32-33
   Sports equipment, 73
St. Mary's County archaeological digs, 86
Sterling, Va., consignment and thrift stores
   Children's clothing, 74
   Clothing, 35
Street vendors
   Downtown opportunities, 139-140
   Roses at a fraction, 102
Summer activities for children, 80-88
Surveys
   Clothing values, consignment vs. retail, 21
   Eating out, reasons for, 1
   Women's work outfits, cost, 21

T

Tag sales, *See* Yard sales
Takoma Park, Md.
   Community Focus, 150-153
   Consignment and thrift stores
     Antiques and collectibles, 151-153
     Children's, 31
     Clothing, 152-153

Music CDs and tapes, 110
House of Musical Traditions, 151
Tall ship, Schooner Alexandria, 158
Theater
    Play previews, 90-91
    Theater in the Woods, Bowie, Md., 149
    Ticket tips, 89-90
    University productions, 90-93; 149
Theme activity weeks, 80-87
Thrift stores
    AmVets and Goodwill locations, 56-57
    Bakery outlets, 16-17
    Description, 44
    Listings, *see* Consignment stores; *specific cities*
Torpedo Factory Arts Center, 157
Toys, 71-74
Trains, 83-84
Trolley Museum at Northwest Branch Regional Park, 84

U
University theater and music productions, 90-93

Used cars, British Embassy list, 123-124
Utilities
    Lighting costs, 58-59
    Time-of-day electric rates, 13-14
    Water for the garden, 67-70

V
Vacation activities for children, 80-88
Valentine's Day
    Classified ads for personal messages, 100
    Flowers and other gifts, 98-102
    Gift baskets, 102
    Heart-shaped cake, 99
    Loveville, Md. postmark, 101
    Velvet roses, 101
Vienna, Va.
    Consignment and thrift stores
        Children's clothing, 74
        Music CDs and tapes, 110
    Nottoway Park Flea Market, 128
Virginia *See specific city, county, or town*

W

Washington, D.C.
  Better Business Bureau, 60
  British Embassy resale list, 122-124
  Consignment and thrift stores
    Books, 119-121
    Children's clothing, 74
    Clothing, 28-30; 137-139; 143
    Collectibles, 138-139
    Furnishings, 56
    General, 137-139
    Music CDs and tapes, 110
  Eastern Market/Capitol Hill, Community Focus, 141-143
  Foggy Bottom/Georgetown, Community Focus, 135-140
  Library system, 87
  Rock Creek Nature Center, 83
  Rosario Center Flea Market, 128
  Street vendors, 139-140
Washington Consumers Checkbook, 62
Washington Monument, 105
Water costs, 67-70
Wedding apparel, 37-41
Wheaton, Md.
  Consignment and thrift stores
    Books, 119
    Clothing, 31
    Music CDs and tapes, 110
  Greeting card outlet, 107
  Trolley Museum at Northwest Branch Regional Park, 84
White House activities
  Greetings Office, 105
  Presidential frugality, 103
Woodbridge, Va., consignment and thrift stores
  Clothing, 34
  Consignment contract, sample, 165-166
  Goodwill store, 57
Wrapping paper, 113-114

Y

Yard sales
  Bethesda, Md., 145
  Books and other treasures, 121-122
  Bowie, Md., 147-148
  Clothing, 43
  Early bird dilemma, 122

Yard sales (Continued)
  Flea markets, 126-129
  House of Representatives, 60
  Stanford A. Tharp collection, 126
  Tips for shopping, 45-46

ABOUT THE AUTHORS

Sarah Crim and Gwen Moulton, two native Washingtonians, conceived the idea for this book while they were both working as reporters for an environmental newsletter. Between them, they have more than 30 years experience as journalists and editors covering an array of topics in the nation's capital.

Ms. Crim and Ms. Moulton for two years edited *The Capital Frugalist* newsletter, and have been interviewed by a wide range of media. Since the early 1990s, they have taught workshops, in corporate and continuing education settings, on how to live thriftily but well in the metro area of Washington, D.C., including suburban Maryland and Virginia.